*f*P

ALSO BY DAVID HOROWITZ

RADICAL SON

SEX, LIES AND VAST CONSPIRACIES

Coauthor of

DESTRUCTIVE GENERATION

DECONSTRUCTING THE LEFT

THE KENNEDYS

THE ROCKEFELLERS

THE FORDS

THE FREE PRESS

NEW YORK   LONDON   TORONTO   SYDNEY   SINGAPORE

DAVID HOROWITZ

The POLITICS *of* BAD FAITH

The Radical Assault On America's Future

*f*P

THE FREE PRESS
A Division of Simon & Schuster Inc.
1230 Avenue of the Americas
New York, NY 10020

THE FREE PRESS and colophon are trademarks
of Simon & Schuster Inc.

Designed by Carla Bolte

Manufactured in the United States of America

1   3   5   7   9   10   8   6   4   2

Library of Congress Cataloging-in-Publication Data
Horowitz, David, 1939–
     The politics of bad faith: the radical assault on America's
future / David Horowitz.
        p.   cm.
     Includes index.
     1. Conservatism—United States.   2. Radicalism—United States.
3. United States—Politics and government—1945–   I. Title.
JC573.H67   1998
320.51'3'097309049—dc21   98-21614
                                                                             CIP

ISBN 0–684–85023–0

TO APRIL

MY PARTNER AND MY PASSION

CONTENTS

INTRODUCTION: THE POLITICAL ARGUMENT REVIVED

THIS BOOK ADDRESSES A CONFLICT THAT FOR TWO HUNDRED years has dominated the political history of the West. It is a conflict that drives America's "culture wars" in the present and that provided the motive force behind the Cold War now past. But it is still referred to in terms that have their origins in the French Revolution, when radicals sat to the left in the National Assembly and their opponents to the right. Many will argue that we have moved beyond these political categories; several books and dozens of articles have appeared bearing the title "Beyond Left and Right," which seek to establish as much. It is widely accepted in the popular culture that we have entered a "post-ideological" age; in the political spectrum, for reasons I will examine, the Left itself has become all but invisible. The argument of this book, however, is that these epitaphs for the conflict that has dominated our epoch are premature: The terms "Left" and "Right" define political forces that have not only shaped modernity but continue to shape the post–Cold War, "postmodern" world. In particular, as I will show in chapter 6, "A Radical Holocaust," the ideas of the Left have dominated the handling of the AIDS epidemic, resulting in the avoidable deaths of hundreds of thousands of young gay males.

IT WAS DURING the French Revolution that the Left created the socialist and communist movements, whose agendas were to "complete" the transformation the revolution had begun. The efforts of these radicals culminated in the Bolshevik Revolution of 1917, whose leaders saw themselves as the direct heirs of Robespierre and the Jacobins, and whose goal was an egalitarian state. But now the empires that socialists built have crashed ingloriously to earth. The catastrophe of the Soviet system has ended for all but the most obdurate the idea that a social plan can replace the market and produce abundance, or that government can abolish private property without also abolishing political freedom.

One might conclude from these facts that the Left is now no more than a historical curiosity, and the intellectual tradition that sustained it for two hundred years is at an end. But if history were a rational process, mankind would have learned these lessons long ago, and rejected the socialist fallacies that have caused such epic grief.

It could also be argued that there has never been a true Right in America, a party committed to monarchy, with religious attachments to "blood and soil." Indeed, as a frontier nation, America has been so future-oriented that, until recently, an American conservatism seemed a contradiction in terms. The contemporary conservative movement emerged only in the 1950s, launching its first presidential bid with the candidacy of Barry Goldwater in 1964. Yet, barely twenty-five years later, the end of Communism had already put the future of this movement in question. Many argued that American conservatism was so much a coalition of convenience—the marriage of disparate philosophies united only by anti-Communist passion—that it would not outlive its ideological adversary.

But the Right has survived its triumphs, even as the Left has outlived its defeats. A few years after the fall of the Berlin Wall, a leader of intellectual conservatism observed: "There is no 'after the Cold War' for me. So far from having ended, my cold war has increased in intensity, as sector after sector of American life has been ruthlessly corrupted by the liberal ethos. It is an ethos that aims simultaneously at political and social collectivism on the one hand, and moral anarchy on the other."[1] What Irving Kristol refers to in this passage as the "liberal ethos" is really not liberal, but the *radical* enterprise that now dresses itself up in "liberal" colors. Group collectivism, racial preferences, "substantive equality" and moral relativism—these are the rallying themes of contemporary liberals. But they have little in common with the liberalism of the pre-Sixties era, or with its classical antecedents. In fact, they make up a radical creed.

Even so, many will contend that today no significant Left exists in America, outside the liberal arts faculties of universities or among the leadership of government unions. They will further claim that the "liberal ethos," to which Kristol refers, is indeed liberal in its agendas, that it aims at no more than a tempering of free-market individualism with social concerns. In this view, the domestic "cold war" is a political chimera, created by the Right to keep its (anti-Communist) faith alive.

It is the argument of this book that such conclusions are misguided. They confuse a momentary equilibrium in the political balance with the deeper forces that shape an epoch. It is true that the Left is rhetorically in retreat and for the moment has adopted more moderate self-descriptions. But that is hardly the same as surrendering its agendas or vacating the field of battle. It is more like adopting a political camouflage on entering a hostile terrain. In the era when Stalin was conquering Eastern Europe, American Communists were calling themselves "progressives" to avoid the taint that Stalinism had inflicted on them. But this was only a protective coloration. It did not involve the slightest change in their real commitments as Marxist radicals, or in their ultimate goals of overthrowing the American government and subverting its Constitution. Far from signaling the end of an anti-American radicalism, as the movements of the Sixties showed, this metamorphosis of Communists into progressives was just the beginning.

It is also true that many liberals, despite sharing a common political front with the Left, are not committed to radical agendas. They are pragmatic enough to tack in a conservative direction should the political wind shift. But by the same token, they are not anchored to any conservative principles that would hold them on course when the same wind shifts again.

Those who question the existence of a Left are influenced, in large part, by an optical illusion created by a culture that is instinctively protective of the Left and that reflects the long-standing dominion of socialist sentiments. In the present post-Communist moment, radicalism is so tainted by its complicity in recent crimes that merely to identify someone as a partisan of the Left would be a damaging accusation. Political bystanders, who may be vaguely sympathetic to leftist ideas or even neutral in the historical debate, will recoil instinctively from the left-wing label as from the stigma of an inquisition. No one wants to be perceived as a "McCarthyist." As a result, even self-avowed Communists like Angela Davis are regularly identified as "liberals" by the media, unless they themselves choose otherwise. The very idiom "to red-bait" shows how ingrained this universal reflex is. There is no comparable term to describe the hostile exposure of loyalties on the Right.

The same protective impulse is manifest in the standards used in public opinion surveys, which are calibrated on scales that range from "liberal" to "conservative" and "ultraconservative," but lack the balance of a "Left." Was the Clinton Administration's attempt to nationalize one-sixth of the economy inspired by socialist illusions? The question may or may not have an affirmative answer. But in the contemporary American culture it is ill-mannered to ask.

A recent report by Americans for Democratic Action shows that forty-seven Democratic House members in the 104th Congress voted to the left of Representative Bernie Sanders, who (alone among them) describes himself as a socialist. An even greater number of politicians who identify themselves as liberal, despite the demise of the socialist bloc, seem to think it unjust that some people earn more than others, a presumption that is the core of leftist belief.

As a result of the prevailing cultural gravity, media arbiters regularly misapply political labels to both sides of the spectrum. Noam Chomsky, the America-loathing MIT socialist is routinely described in the press as a "liberal," while a political adversary like sociologist Charles Murray, who is a libertarian, is normally referred to as "conservative." In the current cultural lexicon, a liberal is thus no longer one who ascribes to the principles of Madison or Locke, or to the institutions of private property and free markets, but to almost anyone who is not labeled a "conservative."

In Europe, by contrast, parties described as "liberal" still reflect the classical origins of the term itself and are associated with economic individualism and free markets. One reason is that in Europe there is a standing socialist tradition that goes back more than a hundred years. It would be inconvenient for radical parties with long socialist histories to suddenly adopt the term "liberal" in order to make a cosmetic adjustment to post-Communist reality. In the United States, however, where the entrance of radicals into the political mainstream has been as recent as the 1970s, such a cosmetic remake is effortless.

For some radicals the term "liberal" is still so distasteful that only the alternatives "progressive" and "populist" are acceptable masks for their chosen agendas. In 1995, *The Nation* magazine printed a manifesto titled "Real Populists Please Stand Up," which read in part:

> We are ruled by Big Business and Big Government as its paid hirelings, and we know it. . . . The big corporations and the centimillionaires and billionaires have taken daily control of our work, our pay, our housing, our health, our pension funds, our bank and savings deposits, our public lands, our airwaves, our elections and our very government. . . . The divine right of kings has been replaced by the divine right of CEOs.[2]

This "populist" vision of America and its ruling class does not differ in any particular from those featured in the Stalinist tracts published in the

1930s, when *The Nation* was a promoter of the Soviet dictatorship and a proud participant in its "Popular Front."

The changes in labeling that have blurred distinctions on the political landscape and obscured the existence of a Left can be traced to the end of the Sixties and the failure of its radical apocalypse. Twenty years earlier, radicals marched out of the Democratic Party to protest its anti-Communist foreign policy and formed the Progressive Party to advance their pro-Soviet agendas behind the presidential candidacy of Henry Wallace. Once having stepped outside the Democratic fold, they shed their liberal masks and, in the Sixties, emerged as New Left radicals condemning both parties as shills for the corporate "ruling class." It was not until the 1972 presidential campaign of former Progressive Party activist George McGovern that the Left returned to its Democratic base.

In making the transition back to the Democratic ranks, radical activists sought to create a fire wall between themselves and their recent careers as political revolutionaries. Without abandoning their old agendas, they sought to escape the taint their leftism had acquired through its resort to violence and its easy embrace of totalitarian causes. They accomplished this, as they had during the Popular Front of the 1930s, by modifying their rhetoric and enveloping themselves in the less threatening mantles of "liberal," "progressive" and "populist."

To acquire even more protective coloration from the political center, socialist radicals coined the term "neoconservative" to describe those adversaries who were genuine liberals opposed to an alliance with the Left. Norman Podhoretz, Irving Kristol and other neoconservative spokesmen have written at length of their efforts to retain the term "liberal" for themselves and preserve the integrity of the political language. But, despite the indisputable logic of their position, they were unable to withstand the dominant influence of the Left in the culture, and the "neoconservative" label stuck.

An ironic result of the Left's success in transforming the lexicon of American politics was that university speech codes and other forms of censorship, in the 1980s, were imposed by people the press identified as "liberals." The authors of these codes were actually the radicals who had entered the academy following the failure of their revolutionary projects in the 1960s. Nor were their opponents, who rejected the idea of "political correctness," really the conservative actors in these campus dramas. By the 1980s, the status quo order at American universities was almost everywhere controlled by the Left. The determined reformers of the censoring regimes were their political opponents on the Right.

A key architect of academic speech codes was radical law professor Catharine MacKinnon, whose theoretical presumptions were laid out in a crude Marxist text, *Toward a Feminist Theory of the State,* and amplified in a tract equating pornography with rape, published by Harvard University Press. In her defense of censorship, Professor MacKinnon revealed how campus commissars were self-consciously carrying on a radical tradition that went back to Marx. "The law of equality and the law of freedom of speech are on a collision course in this country," she announced, expressing the traditional radical disdain for individual rights (free speech) as against group rights (equality). Before the adoption of the Fourteenth Amendment, she continued, "the Constitution contained no equality guarantee." As a result, "the constitutional doctrine of free speech has developed without taking equality seriously—either the problem of social inequality or the mandate of substantive legal equality . . . [entrenched] in the Fourteenth Amendment."[3] According to MacKinnon, the task of legal radicals like herself was to make sure that "substantive" equality was enacted into law, and to embed the principle of equal outcomes in the American constitutional framework.

But neither the doctrine of social equality nor MacKinnon's imaginary "mandate of substantive legal equality" is, in fact, compatible with Madisonian liberalism or with the written Constitution or with the principle of liberty as understood by the American Founders. On the contrary, the "law" of freedom and the "law" of equality were understood by the Framers to be fundamentally in conflict with each other—a conflict that the socialist experiments of the last century have demonstrated with such tragic effect. Whenever a state seeks to enforce "substantive equality" in society, the principles of free speech, private property, and individual freedom inevitably raise insurmountable obstacles to the totalitarian project and are invariably suppressed.

The crypto-Marxist doctrine of "substantive equality," however, is now not limited to radical feminists posturing as liberal academics. What might be called "Fourteenth Amendment Marxism" is a powerful and growing school of jurisprudence on American law faculties,[4] and has profoundly influenced the direction of liberal legal theory in general. In *The Irony of Free Speech,* Owen Fiss, a prominent legal scholar at Yale, advocates the soft version of the MacKinnon doctrine and identifies it with "liberal" jurisprudence as such: "Whereas the liberalism of the Nineteenth Century was defined by the claims of individual liberty and resulted in an unequivocal demand for limited government, the liberalism of today embraces the value of equality as well as liberty." And further: "Today, equality has another place altogether [than it had previously in the American constitutional framework]—it is one of the center beams of the legal order. It is architectonic." By this, Fiss means that "a truly democratic politics will not be achieved until conditions of equality have been fully satisfied."[5] This is the classic Marxist view—the Rights of Man will only be realized in a socialist state. In a typical academic muddle, Fiss proposes to combine the contradictory values, political liberty and equality of condition, ignoring the Founders' explicit recognition of their irresolvable conflict.[6]

More ominous for America's constitutional future is that the doctrine of Fourteenth Amendment Marxism has become the basic charter of the so-called civil rights movement. The presence of the radical agenda in the American mainstream is nowhere more clearly seen than in the battle over the system of racial preferences called "affirmative action." No other issue goes so directly to the heart of America's social contract, to the survival of its pluralist enterprise, or to the shape of its political future.

In November 1997, voters in the largest state in the union overwhelmingly passed the California Civil Rights Initiative, outlawing government preferences and discrimination by race and gender. Known as Proposition 209, the California Civil Rights Initiative was designed to conform to the Civil Rights Act of 1964, prohibiting racial segregation. The words of the initiative are straightforward and simple:

> The state shall not discriminate against, or grant preferential treatment to, any individual or group on the basis of race, sex, color, ethnicity, or national origin in the operation of public employment, public education, or public contracting.

The opposition to this measure was led by the organizations traditionally identified with civil rights that had become radicalized in the preceding decades. The American Civil Liberties Union, the Legal Defense Fund of the NAACP, the AFL-CIO and other opponents of the California Civil Rights Initiative formed a roster of organizations that virtually defined the word "liberalism." When the initiative passed by a 54 percent to 45 percent margin, this liberal coalition appealed to a federal judge for an injunction that would stop its implementation. The initiative, they maintained, was "unconstitutional." The chief litigator for the ACLU called it "the most radical restructuring of the political process to the detriment of minorities in the history of this country"[7]—an indication of just how deep was the division over an understanding of the most basic principle of American pluralism.

In their opposition to the California Civil Rights Initiative, the ACLU-NAACP plaintiffs invoked the Fourteenth Amendment. Drawing on the radical law theories of the academic Left, they argued that it violated the Equal Protection Clause of the amendment. If the courts let the initiative stand, they maintained, it would "impose a special burden on minorities." After hearing the argument, Judge Thelton Henderson granted the injunction. Henderson had been specifically sought out by the plaintiffs to hear the case because he himself was a former left-wing activist and board member of the ACLU. In the ACLU-NAACP complaint, and in Henderson's decision, the radical outlook of the new liberalism could not have been more clearly or more paradoxically expressed: a law *banning* racial preferences was held to violate the Equal Protection Clause, and was therefore regarded as unconstitutional.

The conservative backers of the California Civil Rights Initiative were also veterans of the 1960s civil rights movement, and they appealed Henderson's opinion to the Ninth Circuit Court, where a three-member panel reversed his ruling and lifted the injunction. In reinstating the initiative, the Ninth Circuit found the position of its opponents not only wrong, but incoherent. One could not invoke equal protection of the laws to oppose a law banning racial preferences unless one was in profound disagreement with the constitutional framework itself:

> Proposition 209 amends the California Constitution simply to prohibit state discrimination against or preferential treatment to any person on account of race or gender. Plaintiffs charge that this ban on unequal treatment denies members of certain races and one gender equal protection of the laws. If merely stating this alleged equal protection violation does not suffice to refute it, the central tenet of the Equal Protection Clause teeters on the brink of incoherence.[8]

Not daunted even by this harsh judgment, opponents of the California Civil Rights Initiative announced they would appeal the decision and dig in for a long war. In their appeal, they were joined by the U.S. Department of Justice and the president of the United States.[9] The determination to press the disagreement as a matter of constitutional principle emphasized the radical break that had occurred in the American social contract. A principle that had once been a common foundation for nationhood—equal treatment by the law—had become a ground of fundamental conflict.

The dispute also reflected the distorted terms of political discourse. A law against racial preferences, drafted to conform to the historic civil rights measures of the 1960s, was now "conservative;" opposition to an antidiscrimination law was now "liberal."

The heart of the dispute between liberals and conservatives lay in their opposing views of the Fourteenth Amendment. Did the Equal Protection Clause require government to make its citizens substantively equal (the view of the Left), or did it require government to treat its citizens as equals before the law (the view of the Right). This dispute, of course, engages the entire 150-year history of conflict between Marxist movements, disdainful of "bourgeois rights," and the capitalist democracies of the West. Except that now, the Marxist position is argued by "liberals."

In the debate over the Civil Rights Initiative, the "liberal" side had invoked the provisions of the Fourteenth Amendment as the grounds for striking down the antidiscrimination statute. The Ninth Circuit called this argument "paradoxical," as surely it was. The Fourteenth Amendment had been adopted as a protection for Negroes in the postslavery South who were being stripped by government of their individual civil rights under the infamous "Black Codes." The Fourteenth Amendment was most emphatically *not* designed, as Catharine MacKinnon and the ACLU-NAACP radicals maintained, to guarantee equality for *groups,* whether through government-sponsored affirmative action policies or government programs to redistribute wealth. The Fourteenth Amendment was intended to *prevent* government from discriminating against *individuals,* especially on the basis of race. To underscore this point, the Ninth Circuit, citing a previous Supreme Court decision, observed:

> After all, the "goal" of the Fourteenth Amendment, "to which the Nation continues to aspire," is "a political system in which race no longer matters."

Of course, not everyone opposing the California Civil Rights Initiative was radical in their perspective. Nor is every supporter of affirmative action inspired by the idea of group rights based on race, gender or class. But the principle of group rights is integral to *every* claim for affirmative action preferences, and is antithetic to the most fundamental principles of the American founding. It is the very *un*constitutional idea of "social justice" between groups, which has always been at the heart of the radical project, that now drives much of the political agenda currently described as "liberal." It is this idea that lies behind the attack on America's constitutional framework mounted by "multiculturalists," "critical legal theorists," "critical race advocates," and activist judges who refer to the authority of a "living constitution" unanchored in any written text. The combination of these forces and their pervasive influence in the institutions of American culture and politics, backed by the American presidency, makes the current radical assault on the American founding both formidable and disturbing.

IN ESTABLISHING the proper terms with which to describe this conflict, there remains one final introductory issue, namely, whether the bipolar distinctions "Left" and "Right" still usefully describe the actors themselves. Does this dichotomy accommodate the complexity of views on both sides of the political spectrum? Does the term "Left" really embrace *both* radicals and liberals, and are libertarians properly associated with the Right?

The answers to these questions are, inevitably, both yes and no. While the terms may not be entirely satisfactory in describing complex individual commitments, they are nonetheless indispensable. Left and Right represent distinct and conflicting attitudes toward property, liberty and social equality, which are the axes of contemporary political battles and define their historical possibilities.

On the Right, it is true, the conflicts between libertarians and conservatives remain in many areas fundamental—for example, in those cases where conservatives look to the state to defend the institutions of moral order. But the two parties share a common belief in property as the foundation of human liberty, and a common understanding of the inherent conflict between liberty and equality. These inevitably join them in opposition to the Left.

On the Left, the conflicts between radicals and liberals are less fundamental, concerning means rather than ends. Radicals and liberals share a structure of belief that creates a permanent alliance between them. In *Destructive Generation,* Peter Collier and I attempted to summarize the nature of this alliance in the following formulation: "If the bloodstained reality of the Left is indefensible within the framework provided by liberal principle, its ideals nonetheless seem [to liberals] beyond challenge." We referred to the passage in Lionel Trilling's classic novel *The Middle of the Journey,* where the author makes the same observation:

> Certain things were clear between Laskell and Maxim [Trilling's representative liberal and radical]. It was established that Laskell accepted Maxim's extreme commitment to the future. It was understood between them that Laskell did not accept all of Maxim's ideas. At the same time, Laskell did not oppose Maxim's ideas. One could not oppose them without being illiberal, even reactionary. One would have to have something better to offer and Laskell had nothing better. He could not even imagine what the better ideas would be.[10]

Trilling was referring to ideas like "equality" and "social justice," which define the aspirations of the Left and set their parameters. While not actually supporting Communism, liberals like Laskell were convinced that "one was morally compromised, turned toward evil and away from good, if one was against it." In the conviction that radical goals are noble, however problematic the radical means, lie the seeds of liberalism's historic alliance with—and protection of—the antiliberal Left.

The continuing resonance of this protective attitude can be seen in the loyalties inspired by the Alger Hiss–Whittaker Chambers trial in midcentury, an episode that divided the political culture during the early Cold War. The Roosevelt Administration—the fount of modern American liberalism—had protected Alger Hiss and—wittingly or unwittingly—made it possible for him to function as a Soviet agent and spy. Even after Hiss was proven a traitor, the liberal culture continued to view him as a victim, never the villain of the piece. This attitude of forbearance was extended to the traitor Hiss until the end of his life, after the fall of the Soviet empire, when he was eulogized by liberals—including news anchors for the major networks—as a man who suffered at the hands of dark forces, while gamely maintaining his innocence to the end. His antagonist, on the other hand, the disparaged and long-forgotten Chambers (Trilling's model for the character of Gifford Maxim) was never embraced by liberals as the patriot he was, nor viewed as the hero his service merited. This remained so even after his ideas and actions were vindicated by the fall of Communism and the universal acknowledgment of its terrible crimes.

The alliance between liberals and radicals is reflected throughout a culture that in its deep structures supports the worldview of the Left. This influence is so profound as to have entered the language itself and thus become a habit of mind that is no longer noticed. We speak reflexively of leftists as "progressives," even though their doctrines are rooted in Nineteenth-Century prejudice and have been refuted by a historical record of unprecedented bloodshed and oppression.

In similar fashion, we casually speak of the "haves" and the "have-nots," terms that presume the "social injustice" the Left proposes to redress, while at the same time inflaming the passions of social resentment. Yet, as Friedrich Hayek and others have long pointed out, there is no social entity that divides up society's wealth or can be said to distribute it unjustly. The very term "social justice" describes a prejudice and incitement of the Left, but only this.[11] In a society of liberal politics and economic markets, it would be more appropriate to speak of the "dos" and the "do nots," the "cans" and the "cannots," the "wills" and the "will nots"—terms that reflect the undeniable fact of American social mobility—that individuals can and do make their own destinies, even in circumstances they may not control. Yet, no matter how conservative we may be, we could hardly use these accurate descriptive terms without being simultaneously assaulted by the suspicion that the very usage reflects a mean-spirited attitude on our part which "blames the victim." Such is the power of the political language. To recognize linguistic gravities like these is another way of recognizing the cultural hegemony of the Left.

It is a hegemony with far-ranging social consequences, some of which will be explored in the observations that follow. But our first task is to understand the nature of the radical project, and why it cannot succeed, and thus the reasons that its challenge to democratic order is so dangerous and destructive.

THE ESSAYS IN THIS BOOK explore the trajectory of the radical idea from its origins in the socialist Left to its present incarnation as a movement that calls itself "liberal" and "progressive," but whose ideological agendas are radical and totalitarian. They also necessarily address the interjection of religious ideas into the political arena, a concern normally directed to the "religious Right." Observers as disparate as Berdyaev, Niebuhr, Voegelin, Kolakowski and Talmon long ago, however, recognized and explored the religious dimensions of socialism. The ability of the intellectual Left to survive the catastrophe of its Communist enchantments derives from its essentially religious nature, and reminds us that it is this very attitude, impervious to historical experience and resistant to reason, that remains a durable obstacle to political and social progress.

This book is, finally, about what it means to be a conservative in America, to be "Right" in a context in which conserving the constitutional foundations means defending a fundamentally liberal framework. It seeks to provide a philosophical underpinning for the contemporary conservative coalition that would be broader and more stable than the one that now exists.

The essays were written during and after the fall of the Marxist empire. Three of them—"Unnecessary Losses," "The Road to Nowhere," and "The Religious Roots of Radicalism"—are discussed in my autobiography, *Radical Son,*[12] and are intellectual threads of the odyssey it describes. Although the essays are discrete and self-sufficient, they make up a coherent whole, and are intended to be read in the sequence in which they are presented.

CHAPTER ONE

THE LEFT AFTER COMMUNISM

Workers of the world . . . forgive me.
Karl Marx
—Graffiti on a statue, Moscow 1991

I

THE MONUMENTS HAVE FALLEN NOW AND THE FACES ARE changed. In the graveyards the martyrs have been rehabilitated and everywhere the names have been restored. The Soviet Union, once hailed by progressives everywhere as "one-sixth of mankind on the road to the future," no longer exists. Leningrad is St. Petersburg again. The radical project to change the world has left behind a world in ruin. In a revolutionary eye blink, a bloody lifetime has passed into history. Only vacancies memorialize a catastrophe whose human sum can never be calculated.

In the climactic hours of the Communist fall, someone—Boris Yeltsin perhaps—remarked that it was a pity Marxists had not triumphed

in a smaller country because "we would not have had to kill so many people to demonstrate that utopia does not work." What more is there to
say? If Communism's final hour had truly spelled the end of the utopian
fantasies that have blighted the modern era, nothing at all. If mankind
were really capable of closing the book on this long, sorry episode of human folly and evil, then its painful memory could finally be laid to rest.
Only historians would need to trouble their thoughts over its destructive
illusions and appalling achievements. But, in fact, these millennial
dreams of a brave new world are with us still, and it is increasingly obvious that the most crucial lessons of this history have not been learned.
This observation applies most of all to those whose complicity in its
calamities were most profound—the progressive intelligentsia of the democratic West.

An emblem of this failure was the appearance in 1995 of Eric
Hobsbawm's *Age of Extremes,* a history of the epoch from the outbreak of
the First World War to the end of the Communist empire, which the author refers to as the "short Twentieth Century."[1] *Age of Extremes* is actually the conclusion to a tetralogy of studies that one American reviewer
has called a "*summa historiae* of the modern age,"[2] and which others have
showered with copious accolades since its first volume appeared decades
ago. This final installment was awarded Canada's most coveted literary
prize and appeared to reviews in America that characterized its author's
perspective as canonical for the time. The jacket blurb by a Rockefeller
Foundation executive typically proclaims: "Hobsbawm's magisterial
treatment of the short Twentieth Century will be the definitive *fin-de-
siècle* work." A review in the *New York Times* by Harvard professor Stanley Hoffmann repeats the judgment of the work as "magisterial,"[3] while
liberal foreign policy analyst Walter Russell Mead calls it "a magnificent
achievement of a very rare and remarkable kind."[4] The economist Robert
Heilbroner writes, "I know of no other account that sheds as much light
on what is now behind us, and thereby casts so much illumination on our
possible futures." Hardly less impressed is the historian Eugene Genovese, who reviewed Hobsbawm's book for the *New Republic:*

> We shall soon be flooded with books that seek to explain this blood-drenched century, but I doubt that we shall get a more penetrating and politically valuable one than Eric Hobsbawm's *Age of Extremes*.[5]

These unrestrained encomiums reveal just how deeply embedded in the liberal culture the Marxist paradigm remains, even after the catastrophes it has produced.

For Eric Hobsbawm is himself an emblem. A member of the British Communist Party during the heyday of Stalinism and for decades after, Hobsbawm is today one of the most honored figures in the academic pantheon. He is so—make no mistake—not despite, but *because* of his deplorable past; *because* he continues to be an unrepentant (if moderately chastened) Marxist; because he is a passionate reviler of democratic capitalism, a believer still in thrall to the radical myth. For all Hobsbawm's attention to the details of industrial, scientific and cultural developments in his text, *Age of Extremes* is little more than an ideological tract in behalf of the continuing viability of the socialist faith.

His argument goes like this: Even if "progressives" were wrong, they were right. The practical disasters of socialism should not be taken as a refutation of the socialist idea and its utopian premise.[6] The tragedies produced by socialist revolutionaries are not reasons to abandon the quest for "social justice," or a society based on equality of outcomes and some kind of social plan.

Extravagantly praised by progressive intellectuals for its historical insight, *Age of Extremes* is, in fact, a six-hundred-page apologia for the discredited Left, an advocate's brief for the very project that produced the world of misery under review.

Even more depressing in the way that it reflects our current cultural condition, Hobsbawm's defense of the socialist idea—against all the evidence of its bloodstained reality—is not even original, but repeats an argument first developed by Leon Trotsky during his years of exile, after his fall from grace. According to Trotsky's thesis, Marxism was a design for industrial countries and failed only because its agendas were inserted into a hostile environment for which they were never intended. The cultural and economic backwardness of Russian society thwarted the best-laid plans of the socialist dreamers and produced the distorted result. This is the source of all subsequent arguments from the left that the "actually existing" socialist societies did not represent "true socialism." Following Trotsky's reasoning (but without acknowledging the source), Hobsbawm portrays the Soviet revolution as a forced experiment under unfavorable conditions and thus no test of the ideas that inspired it, or that guided its unhappy results.

In his review of Hobsbawm's book, Professor Hoffmann actually endorses this tired and faulty Communist logic: "Marx was right. . . . socialism could only work in developed countries. . . ." But, of course, Marx was wrong. Otherwise, why would socialism have failed in East Germany, which was the industrial heart of the German Reich until Marxist planners seized its state, destroyed its work ethic and its economic incentives, and ruined its productive base? Neither Hoffmann nor Hobsbawm even attempt to explain this inconvenient historical fact.[7] Moreover, their easy presumption that "Marx was right" about developed countries is unintentionally revealing, since no developed country has ever instituted a successful Marxist "solution."

During the final years of the Soviet empire, socialist economists like John Kenneth Galbraith touted the "success" of Marxist economies and their alleged "convergence" with those of the West. Now that the dismal failure of these societies has been incontrovertibly established, these intellectuals want to forget ever suggesting that the two might be competitive in the first place. Attempting to retrieve a situation shared by sophisticated spokesmen for the Left, Hobsbawm argues that the very idea of a Soviet competition with the West was only an afterthought. It acquired plausibility and became a weapon in the hands of its enemies, because of capitalism's weakness during the Great Depression of the interwar era. In constructing this evasion, Hobsbawm fails to acknowledge the role that Soviet propagandists and Party intellectuals like himself played in fostering this very illusion.

During the Cold War, which Hobsbawm refers to as a "Golden Age" of capitalist development, western economies defied Marxist predictions about ever increasing economic misery and deepening social crisis for reasons Hobsbawm admits he is unable to explain. It was during this expansive era that the industrial democracies of the West were able to permanently surpass the weaker Soviet system, which failed to overcome its economic underdevelopment. Characteristically, it never occurs to Hobsbawm that Marxism itself might be responsible for this failure.

Like other radicals, Hobsbawm writes as though the real-world failures of socialist systems have no implications for socialist critiques of capitalism itself. This denial of the obvious is the intellectual basis for the current survival of the socialist faith and the revival of radical critiques of the West by the political Left. The practice of radical "criticism"—which is a total rejection of the social foundations—is the really destructive dimension of Hobsbawm's work and of the radical culture his ideas reflect. Like his fellow leftists, Hobsbawm's new agenda is to suspend disbelief in the socialist future while extending the socialist indictment of liberal society in the present. In other words, to continue the very assault with which he began his political career seventy years ago, and which led to the monstrous crimes that followed.

One clear indication of the radical passion that inspires Hobsbawm's book is the way it portrays the era of Marxist decline. The eighteen-year period from détente to the Soviet collapse (1973–1991) is described in a section of Hobsbawm's volume called "The Landslide," as though the collapse was caused by a force of nature. Even more revealingly, the term "landslide" is one that Hobsbawm applies to *both* Cold War camps and social systems, as though it described a *global* phenomenon, encompassing East and West. In reality, the period in question witnessed the destruction of the largest and most oppressive empire in recorded history and the spread of democratic governments and market economies around the globe. Yet, through Hobsbawm's Marxist lens, the historic victory of freedom appears as no victory at all, but a general social disintegration on both sides of the ideological divide. The final section of *Age of Extremes* opens with the following summary judgment: "The history of the twenty years after 1973 is that of a world which lost its bearings and slid into instability and crisis."[8]

Though in his own life Hobsbawm is one of its privileged beneficiaries, the triumph of western freedom that resulted from this landslide offers him little satisfaction or relief. In the spacious opening created by the Soviet collapse, the socialist historian sees only "a renaissance of barbarism"—and not just in the post-Communist East, mind you, but in the realm of democracy as well. Socialism has failed, but rather than freedom, it is barbarism that will prevail.

The view that socialism's collapse should be followed by a resurgence of barbarism is less an observation, however, than an ideological *tic*. It reprises the famous call issued by the German Marxist Rosa Luxemburg in the last days of World War I. At that time, Luxemburg summoned the European Left to risk everything in the battle to overthrow the democracies of the West, because the choice before them was "socialism or barbarism." The slogan has been a battle cry for radicals ever since.

If the choice is socialism or barbarism, of course, socialism can still seem attractive to progressives like Hobsbawm. Apocalyptic choice is endemic to the revolutionary equation because it precludes coming to terms with the existing order or entertaining the possibility of piecemeal adjustments and reforms. The elimination of the middle ground justifies in advance the crimes that revolutionaries intend to commit. Before and afterward, it excuses them from drawing a balance sheet of the real-world consequences of their acts.

Eric Hobsbawm is still a prisoner of his reactionary faith. Capitalism remains, in this perversely unshaken ideological perspective, a doomed system, unable to solve its fundamental "crises" except through a revolutionary triumph of the will. As a result, in Hobsbawm's narrative, "capitalism" is depicted as a force of evil—the *diabolus ex machina* of all its tragic turns. In this Manichaean vision, it is democratic America—not its totalitarian adversary—that appears responsible for the fifty-year Cold War. Even the conclusion of that conflict—the Soviet collapse and the Red Army's withdrawal from Eastern Europe—is seen not as a victory for the capitalist West ("We need not take this crusaders' version of the 1980s seriously,"[9] Hobsbawm dismissively writes) but as a victory made possible by the totalitarian enemy itself.

Thus, along with other leftists, Hobsbawm attributes the end of the Cold War to the sagacious policies of the Kremlin's last Communist dictator, who "recognized the sinister absurdity of the nuclear arms race" and approached his antagonists with a proposal to end it: "That is why the world owes so enormous a debt to Mikhail Gorbachev, who not only took this initiative but succeeded, single-handed, in convincing the US government and others in the West that he meant what he said."[10] Gorbachev was able to achieve this near miraculous resolution of the Cold War, according to Hobsbawm, only because the White House—normally a center of war-mongering paranoia—was occupied by a simpleton who remained immune from its most malignant influences:

> However, let us not underestimate the contribution of President Reagan whose simple-minded idealism broke through the unusually dense screen of ideologists, fanatics, careerists, desperadoes and professional warriors around him to let himself be convinced.[11]

This is a maliciously absurd cartoon of American government that only other leftist intellectuals could credit. What a world of difference between Hobsbawm's account and the actual gratitude expressed for America's cold warriors and above all for their leader, Ronald Reagan, by the people they liberated from the Soviet yoke. In the aftermath of the Cold War, the multitudes behind the former Iron Curtain regarded Ronald Reagan as their champion, while Hobsbawm's hero, Gorbachev, became a man forgotten and without a following even in his own country.

Throughout his narrative of the Cold War's denouement, Hobsbawm remains oblivious to a factor of momentous consequence underlying both the Soviet collapse and the triumph of the West. This factor was the power of private markets to unleash new technologies and to transform the economic world, while socialist planners were unable to do the same. In a four-hundred-page volume that devotes entire chapters to scientific and industrial developments, Hobsbawm mentions the digital computer only in passing and then only in a single isolated sentence. There is not a single reference to Seymour Cray, Bill Gates, Larry Ellison, Jim Clark, Michael Milken or any of the other Rockefellers and Fords behind the new industrial revolution or—except negatively—to the economic and social implications of this epoch-making event.

Hobsbawm first ignores and then denies the liberating potential of the computer-driven revolution, as he does the greatest peacetime expansion in history—the Reagan boom of the Eighties—which helped to launch it. Instead, his portrait of America's economy in the prospering Eighties is one of unrelieved foreboding and social gloom. Like a modern-day Luddite who has learned nothing from two hundred years of industrial innovation, Hobsbawm receives the news of technological progress as a social threat. In Hobsbawm's doom-ridden scenario, technological progress means only the prospect that jobs will be eliminated—forever:

> The Crisis Decades [1973 to the present] began to shed labor at a spectacular rate, even in plainly expanding industries. . . . The number of workers diminished, relatively, absolutely and, in any case, rapidly. The rising unemployment of these decades was not merely cyclical but structural. The jobs lost in bad times would not come back when times improved: they would never come back.[12]

As this Marxist reactionary returns to the myths of his radical youth, he imagines the capitalist past conjured in those myths to be recurring eternally in the capitalist present: "In the 1980s and early 1990s the capitalist world found itself once again staggering under the burdens of the inter-war years, which the Golden Age appeared to have removed: mass unemployment, severe cyclical slumps, the ever-more spectacular confrontation of homeless beggars and luxurious plenty. . . ." To this structural dislocation, Hobsbawm attributes a "growing culture of hate" and a general social breakdown (including an alleged epidemic of "mass murders") that cloud the American future.[13] In other words, Marx's predictions of increasing misery, increasing polarization of rich and poor, increasing crisis—were right.

But only in the fantasies of an unreconstructed believer in the radical faith. In reality, during the decades of the Cold War, the engines of capitalist progress were revolutionizing the lives of ordinary working people on a scale previously inconceivable. Hobsbawm's "landslide" in the West coincided with economic developments that ushered in the greatest social transformation in human history—the first time in five thousand years that more than a tiny percentage of the population of any society were able to attain a degree of material well-being. It was, in fact, this dazzling prospect of American progress in the era that stretched from Eisenhower to Reagan that lay at the heart of the demoralization and collapse of socialism's empire, whose own populations had been condemned to permanent grinding poverty by Marx's impossible economic schemes. Over the course of Hobsbawm's somber decades, the consumption of goods and services by the average American family had actually doubled. While less than 10 percent of Americans went to college in 1950, almost 60 percent had done so by 1996. By that time, the poorest fifth of the population was consuming more than the middle fifth in 1955.[14] None of this uplifting reality—a liberation of the dispossessed that no socialist state ever accomplished—is allowed to penetrate Hobsbawm's unrelenting negative vision.

Age of Extremes—so readily embraced by the liberal culture—is little more than an elaborate and pathetic defense of the two destructive illusions in whose name the Left has caused so much suffering in the Twentieth Century: the inherent evil of capitalist society and the humanitarian promise of the socialist future. In the wake of the Soviet disaster, of course, the hope of this socialist future is only tenuously put forward by sophisticated radicals like Hobsbawm. It is the negative assault on democratic capitalism that inspires their commitment and that leads their public agenda. In the permanent war of the Left against liberal economy and democratic order, it is understood by radicals that offense is always the best defense.

But the two sides of the radical argument cannot really be separated. The nihilistic rejection of the present order is necessarily predicated on the dream of a redemptive solution. Inevitably, in the closing passage of Hobsbawm's text, the two ideas are finally linked. And they are linked in a manner that is as intellectually extreme as any manifesto by Rosa Luxemburg or Karl Marx:

> The forces generated by the techno-scientific economy are now great enough to destroy the human environment, that is to say, the material foundations of human life. . . . We have reached a point of historic crisis. . . . If humanity is to have a recognizable future, it cannot be by prolonging the past or the present. If we try to build the third millennium on that basis we shall fail. And the price of failure, that is to say the alternative to a changed society, is darkness.

Capitalist darkness or revolutionary light. Socialism or barbarism. Like the Bourbons of the Nineteenth Century, the reactionaries of the contemporary Left have learned nothing from this history, and they have forgotten nothing either.

II

The radical idea has not been buried with its hapless victims, nor the fantasy of a world redeemed. Yet, it is this very hope that provides the impetus for atrocity, the golden omelet for which it has seemed reasonable to progressive minds to break so many eggs.

In the aftermath of the Nazi Holocaust, no intellectual calling himself progressive would have ignored the link between the racist idea and the "final solution." But no progressive intellectual today will recognize the parallel nexus between the socialist idea and the gulags it produced.[15] To the progressive mind, the idea remains innocent and the Soviet tragedy only a temporary detour from the path of socialist progress. In this view, "actually existing socialism" bears no relation to the socialist promise. The failure of Marxism can be dismissed as the result of an intellectual error that progressives have already corrected.

There is a sense, of course, in which even nonsocialists might view this entire episode of a failed utopia as an epic mistake. Few intellectual doctrines have been so systematically refuted—over so many generations—as the socialist vision of Karl Marx. None has been the cause of so much human misery and suffering. Yet false doctrines of this proportion are not sustained by ignorance alone. Throughout the history of the Marxist faith, there has never been a lack of first-rate intellectuals to validate its "truths," or to lend reputation and talent to its most malignant agendas: to lie when it was necessary to lie; to believe when it should not have been possible to believe; to justify murder and defend what is indefensible.

> It will always be a mark of moral and intellectual dishonor for the West that in this historic and protracted encounter with the adversaries of freedom and democracy so many of our most gifted writers, artists, scientists, and intellectuals were more energetically engaged in opposing our own political institutions and the ideas essential to their survival than in questioning either the lethal political doctrines that were designed to destroy them or the elaborate edifice of cultural mendacity that was spawned by the Communist movement for the express purpose of bringing down the democratic societies of the West.[16]

The socialist experiments of the Twentieth Century ruined the economies of whole continents and destroyed the lives of hundreds of millions, all with the acquiescence and support of intellectuals who thought of themselves as progressive. When the experiments were over, these progressives were faced with an existential choice. On the one hand, they could confront their complicity in socialist crimes and give up the illusion that made them inevitable. In short, they could abandon the Left. Or, like Eric Hobsbawm, they could renew the illusion and get on with their war against the democracies of the West.

In the years following the Communist collapse, the vast majority of progressive intellectuals chose the second course. Perhaps it was too difficult to admit lifelong error and acknowledge the rectitude of one's hated opponents. Perhaps it meant traumas to the soul for which they were not prepared. In any case, it was easier to avoid than to face unpleasant truth. But this avoidance was possible only through an act of historical denial—psychologically speaking, a progressive bad faith.

Two principal strategies were employed in the pursuit of this denial.

The first was that adopted by Communist diehards in the former Soviet states, who viewed the collapse of Communism as a failure of those attempting its reform. In their eyes, Communism was not vanquished by a superior system; it was surrendered by its own leaders who lost their revolutionary nerve. A variation of the theme argues that Gorbachev's reforms were unwisely implemented. The destabilizing political reforms of *glasnost* should have been attempted only *after* the economic reforms of *perestroika* were put in place. This would have left the Communists in control, as in China.

The second, more prevalent, strategy of denial is dependent on a "postmodernist" attitude that accepts the fact of Communist failure while avoiding its implications. This strategy acknowledges the failure of existing socialism, while denying its connection to the radical project. In the words of one Marxist academic, "The nightmare is over, the dream lives on."[17] As though the nightmare was not also the dream. This form of denial is the path taken by most of the intellectuals who have remained faithful to the progressive idea.

It is easy to see why this should be the strategy of choice. Once the postmodern ellipsis is achieved—once the connection with history is lost—the epistemological problem of a progressive faith disappears. One no longer has to trouble oneself about the actual reasons for the Soviet collapse. Or whether the socialist idea is to blame. To free oneself from the moral consequences of the socialist fate, one has only to suspend belief in the socialist idea. Then one can proceed to the revolt against capitalist society as though nothing of consequence had occurred. As though the Cold War had ended in defeat but no victory. This is the preferred perspective of Hobsbawm's text and of his comrades in the post-Communist Left.

It is a posture that was on full display at a June 1990 forum held by the Organization of American Historians (one of innumerable academic associations now controlled by this Left). The topic of the forum was "Who Won the Cold War?" During the discussion, the social critic Christopher Lasch raised the need for second thoughts: "We ought to admit the truth . . . that the West won the Cold War, even if it does go against the grain, against our political inclinations." Lasch's candid admission was dismissed by the leftist academics with outrage and scorn. Observing the proceedings, E. J. Dionne of the *Washington Post* reported that those in attendance "were firm in their view that the revolutions in Eastern Europe had done nothing to vindicate [the West]." Lasch was attacked for justifying a "heroic view of America's world role."[18]

The refusal to confront the past meant that leftists could resume their attacks on America and the West without examining the movements and regimes they had supported, and thus without proposing any practical alternative to the societies they continued to reject. The intellectual foundations of this destructive attitude had already been created, in the preceding decades, in a development that Allan Bloom described as the "Nietzscheanization of the Left"[19]—the transformation of the progressive faith into a nihilistic creed.

Nihilistic humors have always been present in the radical character. The revolutionary will, by its very nature, involves a passion for destruction alongside its hope of redemption. While the hope is vaguely imagined, however, the agenda of destruction is elaborate and concrete. It was Marx who originally defended this vagueness, claiming that any "blueprint" of the socialist future would be merely "utopian," and therefore should be avoided. The attitude of the post-Marxist Left is no different. Since the fall of Communism, radical intellectuals have continued their destructive attacks on capitalism, as though the catastrophes they had recently promoted posed no insurmountable problem to such an agenda. "I continue to believe," wrote a radical academic after the Soviet collapse, "that what you call 'the socialist fantasy' can usefully inform a critique of post-modern capitalism without encouraging its fantasists and dreamers to suppose that a brave new order is imminent or even feasible."[20]

But how could a responsible intellect ignore the destructive implications of such an attitude? The socialist critique, after all, is total. It is aimed at the roots of the existing order. To maintain agnosticism about the futures that might replace the reality you intend to destroy may be intellectually convenient, but it is also morally corrupt.

"Critical theory"—the coy self-description of the ideological Left—

self-consciously defines itself by the totality of its rejection of the existing social order, in identical fashion to old-style Marxists (Marx himself was a "critical theorist"). The explicit agenda of critical theory is to undermine the credibility and authority of the status quo in order to prepare its annihilation. The task of undermining communal assumptions and stabilizing faiths is not incidental to the radical critique, but is its corrosive essence. It is what the theory *intends*. Yet, like the Marxist-Leninists of the past, critical theorists never confront the moral issue posed by their destructive agendas: *What can be the rationale for weakening and ultimately destroying a system as liberal as the existing one, if no better has been devised?*

Without its adherents noticing, the theoretical argument of the Left has been emptied of content by the failures of socialism. For what is the practical meaning of a socialist critique in the absence of a workable socialist model? In fact, there is none. By adopting an impossible standard, it is easy to find fault with any institution or social system under scrutiny. The ideal of socialist equality, for example, may or may not be admirable. But if social equality cannot be realized in practice, or if the attempt to realize it necessarily creates a totalitarian state, then the idea of such equality can have no significance *except* as an incitement to destructive agendas.

To raise the socialist ideal as a critical standard imposes a burden of responsibility on its advocates that critical theorists refuse to shoulder. If one sets out to destroy a lifeboat because it fails to meet the standards of a luxury yacht, the act of criticism may be perfectly "just," but the passengers will drown all the same. Similarly, if socialist principles can only be realized in a socialist *gulag,* even the presumed inequities of the capitalist market are worth the price. If socialist poverty and socialist police states are the practical alternative to capitalist inequality, what justice can there be in destroying capitalist freedoms and the benefits they provide? Without a practical alternative to offer, radical idealism is radical nihilism—a war of destruction with no objective other than war itself.

To confront the catastrophe of the radical vision requires moral effort, but the nihilistic pose that evades the issue requires no exertion at all. "Postmodern" leftism—the theoretical expression of agnostic nihilism—makes it possible for progressives to keep the radical faith without undertaking a painful inventory of the radical achievement. That is why, for the contemporary Left, it has become the ideology of choice: the postmodern attitude relieves progressives of any obligation to acknowledge their complicity in radical crimes. It makes it possible to preserve one's political identity while maintaining the semblance of self-respect. This is what makes nihilism the preferred perspective for Hobsbawm and other intellectuals who want to be faithful to the bankrupt traditions of the Left, while earning moral credit for acknowledging "mistakes." The post-Communist Left is too shrewd to defend a future that has so comprehensively failed. But it seeks to retrieve its catastrophes by pretending that the failure doesn't matter.

To the contemporary Left, those who did fail, who actually committed socialist crimes have no relationship to *them*. The response of the Left to the disasters that its political ideas have produced is the response of nihilism and bad faith.

This bad faith has been rationalized by a new generation of academic intellectuals who have opened a Pandora's box of radical theories that are derivative of Marxism while pretending to transcend it. The edifice of the new "critical" theory is supported by an intellectual posture that pretends to be skeptical and/or relativist about everything except itself (an analytic self-deception that it shares with Marxism).

By the time the *gulag* collapsed in Russia, the very truth that Stalin and his commissars had worked so hard to suppress by rewriting history and silencing its witnesses had virtually vanished as a concept among progressive intellectuals. French "deconstructionist" ideas about the "aporia" of discourse and the indeterminacy of language, "poststructuralist" and "postmodernist" assaults on the idea of the historical subject, and "antifoundationalist" and Foucauldian critiques of the objectivity of knowledge—all reducing truth to communal prejudice and convenience of power—have made the evasions of an entire radical generation seem hardly devious or even hypocritical. More like a convenient wisdom. This intellectual bait-and-switch operation was accomplished largely by grafting Nietzsche onto Marx and turning the "materialist science of history" into a hollow and corrosive cynicism. Eventually, it became difficult—in the smug summation of one left-wing philosopher—to find "a real live metaphysical prig" on the faculties of American universities; that is, someone who believed in "reality" and "truth."[21]

Was it mere accident that relativism and its twin, nihilism, should become outlooks of the Left at the precise moment that its ideas were being refuted by historical events? Or was this, rather, the most efficient way to avoid the painful but necessary meanings of its past—the truth of progressives' complicity in the most terrible crimes of the century? In retrospect, the deconstructionist "turn" and its doctrinal bedfellows formed a necessary answer to the radical dilemma: How to avoid the truth of a history that had punctured its utopian illusion, while continuing on with its radical adventure. How to maintain the destructive passions of the radical idea in the face of the failure of its radical project. By disestablishing the integrity of any and every historical narrative, progressive intellectuals provided themselves with an ingenious (dis)solution.

Utopianism and nihilism, of course, are but two sides of the same intellectual coin. Revolution, as conceived by the secular messianists of the modern Left, is really the vision of a new creation. But the creative work of every revolution begins as a work of destruction, and its creed is the cry of Goethe's Mephistopheles: *All that exists deserves to perish.*[22] The revolutionary imperative follows: to sever the past from the future, to annihilate what has been for what will be—*Aufhebung*—to deconstruct, de-structure, de-mystify, dis-solve, demolish, defame, debase, deny; to create out of something, nothing. Nowhere.

And what is the world that is to be denied and destroyed by the contemporary Left, with its deconstructionist agendas, but (once again) the democratic societies of the capitalist West. Is it an accident that the seminal thinkers of the postmodern Left are the Twentieth Century's destructive utopians, namely, Communists and Nazis: Heidegger, de Man,

Gramsci, Lukács, Althusser, and Foucault? Or that their Nineteenth-Century intellectual godfathers are Nietzsche and Marx? "Every anti-liberal argument influential today," as the political philosopher Stephen Holmes has written, "was vigorously advanced in the writings of European fascists," including the critique of "its atomistic individualism, its myth of the pre-social individual, its scanting of the organic, its indifference to community . . . its belief in the primacy of rights, its flight from 'the political,' its decision to give abstract procedures and rules priority over substantive values and commitments, and its hypocritical reliance on the sham of judicial neutrality."[23]

Or, to cite another authority: "Cultural determinism, the reduction of all social relationships to issues of sheer power; the idea that one's identity is centered in one's ethnicity or race; the rejection of the concept of the individual . . . all of these ideas are direct echoes of the fascist theorists of the 1930s."[24] Of course, only the Left could get away with resurrecting the theories of European fascism, while labeling itself "progressive" in the process.

Is it surprising that discredited Marxism still provides the paradigm for every current radical ideology from feminism to queer theory? Or that the totalitarian attitudes endemic to Marxism are also everywhere in evidence in the academic discourse of the tenured Left? The literary critic Harold Bloom describes in horror the current political trends in the university as "Stalinism without Stalin." "All of the traits of the Stalinists in the 1930s and 1940s are being repeated . . . in the universities in the 1990s."[25]

These ironies are reflected in the required texts of Columbia's Contemporary Civilization course, the nation's oldest, relatively undeconstructed, liberal-arts curriculum. Columbia's new canon is an attempt to establish an orthodoxy out of the very intellectual tradition that history has refuted. Only two Nineteenth-Century thinkers are represented in the course who are *not* socialists—Max Weber and Charles Darwin. For the arbiters of the new canon, it is as if the intellectual tradition of free-market liberalism had ended in the Eighteenth-Century with Madison,

Smith and Locke. When the Columbia course enters the Twentieth-Century, no dissent at all is tolerated. The required texts are exclusively by left-wing intellectuals, including Jürgen Habermas and John Rawls, the Communists Antonio Gramsci and Lenin, the Stalinist camp follower Simone de Beauvoir, and the violent racialists Frantz Fanon and Malcolm X. The required curriculum is filled out by two second-rate ideologues, Catharine MacKinnon and Cornel West.[26] Even the course's lone authority on totalitarianism, Hannah Arendt, a distinguished intellectual and Social Democrat, was a disciple of Heidegger.[27] As far as the contemporary academy is concerned, the intellectual tradition that informed the American founding, whose disciples in the Twentieth Century led the battle against totalitarian ideology and socialist economics—von Mises, Hayek, Aron, Popper, Berlin, Bloom, Friedman, Strauss—provides an unworthy model for America's future elites. The contemporary academy prefers the paradigms, the avatars, and the fellow travelers of the discredited Left instead.

This transformation of the curriculum did not happen by accident but was the calculated result of a twenty-year political assault on America's institutions of higher learning. These attacks ranged from armed intimidation at Cornell in the Sixties to ugly demonstrations at Stanford in the Eighties. Their common purpose was to politicize the curriculum and infuse it with left-wing agendas. At Stanford, the demonstrators were led by the Reverend Jesse Jackson in a protest against the course in Western Civilization required of all undergraduates and modeled on Columbia's core curriculum. Jackson led the demonstrators in a summary chant: *"Hey, hey, ho, ho, Western Civ has got to go!"*

In the wake of these protests, Western Civ—a course designed to introduce students to the works of Aristotle, Plato, St. Augustine, Dante, Shakespeare and other great figures of western culture—did go. It was replaced by a new curriculum called simply "CIV." Defenders of the new curriculum attempted to disarm critics by disingenuously claiming that the changes did not mean that Western Civilization would no longer be taught (many original texts in fact remained) but only that previously excluded cultures and readings would now be included. But the claim was empty because the mission of the university had already changed and along with it the way in which even the old canon was taught.

Instead of a course devoted to the great shaping moral and intellectual traditions of the West, the values that have made its culture the fount of modern technology and science, of market economics and democratic politics, the new course was designed to indoctrinate students into the peculiar Marxoid worldview that had come to characterize the academic Left. (One typical new title, for example, was the autobiography of a Maoist spokeswoman for Guatemalan guerrillas, written under the guidance of a Parisian leftist, called *I, Rigoberta Menchú.*)[28] The catalogue description of the CIV course made it clear that its purpose would no longer be to introduce students to the crowning achievements of western culture, but would inculcate a specific, left-wing, ideological viewpoint. According to the catalogue, the course would teach:

- the ways in which class and gender shape human life
- construction of group identities
- the conflict between freedom and equality[29]

Instead of being instilled with the values and ideas that have made the West the cradle of global modernity, students would be drilled in the primary structures of the Left's discredited worldview. If class and gender "shape human life" (as the course presumes), and if group identities are socially "constructed," the conflict between freedom and equality can only be resolved by Marxist and totalitarian solutions.[30]

And this is, in fact, the way the CIV course is taught at Stanford. The official course outline for Professor Renato Rosaldo's "Europe and the Americas" track in the 1988 CIV sequence, for example, reads as follows:

First quarter: The Spanish debate over indigenous rights raises issues around race as well as religion; readings on European enlightenment include Wollstonecraft on question of gender, and Flora Tristan on question of class. Race, gender and class are all thematized in Chungara de Barrios' autobiography and Anzaldúa's poetic essays. Second quarter: Race is a central focus of materials on the Haitian revolution, and materials from the twentieth century negritude movement which developed in the post-emancipation context of modern "scientific" racism. Gender is a central issue in Jamaica Kincaid's novel "Annie John," a mother-daughter story. Roumain's "Masters of the Dew" plays out a class drama around the conflict between traditionalist peasant culture and modern proletarian consciousness. Third quarter: Marx and Weber are essential sources on class; Frantz Fanon on race; gender, ethnicity and class are central themes in Rulfo, Menchú, Chavez and Anzaldúa.[31]

Clearly, this is no longer an introduction to the great enriching themes of western culture, but a course in the way Marxist categories can be used to define social realities and construct revolutionary agendas.

Of all the influences on contemporary academic radicals, Martin Heidegger's may be the most psychologically revealing. Heidegger's influence derives partly from his importance to academic theory generally, but also from the fact that he has directly influenced seminal leftists like Derrida, Foucault and Sartre. As a Nazi, Heidegger's socialist utopia was national in character, but his response to its implementation in the Third Reich is strikingly reminiscent of Marxist responses to the revealed horrors of the Soviet state. In Heidegger's postwar refusal to recant his Nazi commitments, he anticipated the denials later employed by American leftists refusing to discard their parallel faith.

The first and most important of these was to reject the possibility that the fate of the actually existing Nazi state reflected in any way on the ideas that created it. In a postwar correspondence with Herbert Marcuse, Heidegger wrote: "Your letter just shows how difficult a dialogue is with people . . . who evaluate the beginning of the National Socialist movement from the perspective of its end." Thus did Heidegger seek to sever historical practice from its intellectual foundations, to distance himself from actually existing Nazism while preserving his fealty to the Nazi ideal. Even after the Holocaust, Heidegger continued to defend this ideal, much as the socialist ideal is still defended by the western Left. In these postures, Heidegger appeared as a kind of German Trotsky, complaining that the Nazi rulers had betrayed "the inner truth and grandeur of National Socialism,"[32] as though that truth were not implicated in the deeds of those who lived by it.

To the believer, the practice that fails is necessarily a "betrayal" of the utopian intentions; it is never a reflection of the idea itself. Thus, Samuel Bowles, a Marxist professor at the University of Massachusetts, responded to the news of the Soviet collapse with a bald evasion typical of his radical peers: "Like many other leftist academics, I am frequently asked these days 'How are you coping with the dethroning of Marxism and the demise of Communism in Eastern Europe?' I am not alone in responding: 'It's the end of a nightmare, not the death of a dream' . . ." As though the one were not contained in the other.

The second mode of denial favored by western Marxists and Nazis like Heidegger is the doctrine of moral equivalence, which is simply a form of nihilism. This is an attitude that refuses to distinguish between actually existing totalitarian socialisms and the liberal realities of capitalist states. The source of this otherwise inexplicable lacuna is the utopian illusion. For the socialist believer, the defects of socialism are dwarfed by its potential to blossom into human freedom, while the defects of capitalism are magnified by the perception that it stands in the way of the socialist dream.

Because the revolutionary project requires the total condemnation of the present order, extreme or isolated examples of capitalist evils are ritually invoked by radicals as typifying its reality. In an attempt to rationalize his Nazi illusions to Herbert Marcuse, for example, Heidegger made the following appeal:

> To the severe and justified reproach that you express "over a regime that has exterminated millions of Jews, that has made terror a norm and that transformed everything connected to the concepts of spirit, freedom, and truth into its opposite," I can only add that instead of the "Jews" one should put the "East Germans," and that is even the case for one of the Allied Powers, with the difference that everything that happened since 1945 is known to

all the world, while the bloody terror of the Nazis in reality was kept secret from the German people.

In Heidegger's equation, the crime of the Holocaust is morally canceled by the mistreatment of East Germans during the liberation of Europe. In similar fashion, leftists in America regularly invoke and conflate the dropping of the atomic bomb at Hiroshima, the lynching of 3,000 Negroes over a hundred-year period in the segregationist South, and atrocities committed during the Vietnam War to equate liberal America with totalitarian and racist states. In rationalizing his political loyalty to the Third Reich (despite its "betrayal" of the Nazi ideal), Heidegger anticipated most of the rationalizations the Left would use in defending its sympathies for the Communist bloc. "Russia and America," he claimed in the 1935 *Introduction to Metaphysics,* "are both . . . the same; the same wretched mad rush of unbridled technology and the same unbounded organization of the average human being." A similar equation came to function as a Cold War formula of the western Left. It was epitomized in the fatuous remark of sometime Maoist Michel Foucault: "What could politics mean when it was a question of choosing between Stalin's USSR and Truman's America?"[33] What indeed!

Where rationalization fails the believer, silence—the refusal to confront the actual consequences of belief—is the refuge of last resort. Heidegger's silence was maintained for the last forty years of his life. He never attempted to trace the progress of the ideal in its practice, to connect the ideas of National Socialism with their actual results. This subterfuge is reprised in the history of the post-Communist Left. No left-wing theorist has seriously confronted the origins of Stalinism in Lenin and Marx, or come to terms with the fact that *every* successful Marxism resulted in a totalitarian state.

By these intellectual maneuvers, radicals have been able to resurrect the utopian vision and the destructive enterprise it engenders. The perfect future is once again invoked to condemn the imperfect present. As Nietzsche observed, "Idealism kills." Without the noble utopian idea, the evil practice would not exist.

AT THE MOMENT of Communist collapse, the bankrupt vision of a Marxist utopia was defended by Sam Bowles with the argument that "Marx wrote almost nothing about socialism or communism." According to Bowles, the collapse of socialism indicated the need for a lot of "rethinking about socialist economies but little about capitalist economies."[34] Bowles's posture became the common attitude of radical intellectuals defending their position. But no critique exists independently of the standard that informs it. Bowles's defense merely rehashes Heidegger's contention that Nazism should not be judged from the perspective of its result. The statement, moreover, manifests a profound ignorance of the nature of Marxism and the intellectual foundations of its anticapitalist critique: far from ending with the hypothesis of a socialist solution, Marxism *begins* with it.[35] The entire edifice of Marx's indictment of class society depends on the possibility of transcending class society, of replacing capitalism with a planned economy—the very idea that has now been refuted by historical events.

This is made clear in the opening chapter of *Capital,* in a section titled "The Fetishism of Commodities and Its Secret," which contains the most influential statement of Marx's critique. It provides the conceptual basis not only for Marx's economic argument, but for all Marxist cultural theories, which are little more than a series of footnotes to the discussion of reification in these pages. "Cultural studies," the recently created academic field for the exfoliation of Marxist ideas centered in this passage, is now perhaps the last flourishing socialist industry.

In this seminal argument, Marx defines capitalism as a "commodity producing society" and asks: "Whence . . . arises the enigmatical character of labor's product, so soon as it assumes the form of commodities?" For Marx, the answer is found in private property and the economic market.[36] The commodity form creates the conditions in which labor's "own social action takes the form of the action of objects, which rule the producers instead of being ruled by them." It is this fetishism of the object, produced by capital, which allegedly robs mankind of its powers and alienates the producer from the product of his labor. Commodities thus produce the characteristic form of oppression of capitalist societies. How does

Marx propose to overcome the servitude caused by the fact that the producers are alienated from their own power? The answer is: by a social plan.

> The life-process of society, which is based on the process of material production, does not strip off its mystical veil until it is treated as production by freely associated men, and is consciously regulated by them in accordance with a settled plan.[37]

An association of the producers to plan the economic life of society is Marx's solution to the riddle of human history. It is also precisely what the vast carnage and human waste of the "Soviet experiment" has proved impossible. The very idea of the Left is bankrupt along with the socialist state.

BUT THE ACTUAL Left refuses to die. Even though the collapse of Communism produced a momentary caesura in the radical promotion of the socialist faith, there has been no retreat from left-wing theory and—more important—no abatement in left-wing attacks on the democracies of the West. In the very month the Berlin Wall was being torn down, American radicals were being urged by the editors of *The Nation* not to be paralyzed by doubts about the socialist future, but "to get on with the job. . . . [The Left] must attack the very foundation of our own system."[38] To get on with the "job." In other words *to get on with the task of destruction.* This is what the radical project is about.

From the redoubts of its academic stronghold, the Left has been getting on with the task of destruction for nearly three decades. It has systematically purged conservative scholars and theories from the academic environment and institutionalized views of America's history, traditions and political ideals that are as unrelenting in their hostility to American purpose, and their condemnation of American achievement, as any article in *New Masses* or *Pravda* or in the collected volumes of the Little Lenin Library.

Consider this representative outburst in a legal text by Robin West, one of the foremost academic feminists and a professor of constitutional law at Georgetown University. In the passage, Professor West expresses her feelings about the Constitution she has been entrusted to teach, as well as the history of the nation it created:

> The political history of the United States that culminated and is reflected in the constitutional text is in large measure a history of almost unthinkable brutality toward slaves, genocidal hatred of Native Americans, racist devaluation of nonwhites and nonwhite cultures, sexist devaluation of women, and a less than admirable attitude of submissiveness to the authority of unworthy leaders in all spheres of government and public life. Why should we bind or constrain our political argument, to say nothing of our political choices, by texts produced by this history of ruthlessness; of brutality; and of mindless, infantile, and at times psychotic, numbing wrath?[39]

It is a sober thought that the author of this rant is representative of a major school of "progressive" jurisprudence in the nation's elite law faculties.[40]

Through "multicultural" assaults on western culture, and on the political communities dominated by "white males" that created America's institutions, the radical work of deconstructing the very idea of American nationality is well advanced. Parallel assaults on American society and institutions by academic Marxists, critical race theorists, and radical feminists have made the work of defaming the narrative of freedom and replacing it with a saga of blood conquest and racial oppression equally familiar. The new American heritage constructed by academic radicals can hardly nourish that "reverence for the sources of our being" that Santayana identified with patriotism. Quite the opposite. But, then, that is the very aim of the radical agenda—to sever those loyalties that would tie America's emerging elites to their country. Such alienation, which includes the will to abrogate and then rewrite the Constitution, is the essential element without which the agenda of revolution is not possible.

THE MAJORITY OF those who inhabit the progressive culture would perhaps shrink from such baldly expressed anti-American agendas.

Yet, these intellectual fellow travelers are also the willing accomplices of the radicals who advance them. Consider the case of Richard Rorty, one of the nation's most prominent academic philosophers. The son of a leading American Trotskyist, Rorty describes himself as a "democratic socialist" with a soft spot for the virtues of existing bourgeois rights. As a voice of moderation in the academic Left, Rorty provides an instructive example of the way the totalitarian temptation survives in the heart of the culture, even after Communism's collapse. Though he is the nation's leading philosophic skeptic, Rorty is still hooked on the utopian illusion, with all its destructive implications.

Shortly after the Soviet debacle, Rorty was attacked in the academic journal *Transition* for his deviant appreciation of bourgeois virtues. The attack was launched by his own disciple, Harvard professor and self-styled "prophetic thinker" Cornel West, who expressed his dissatisfaction with Rorty's "fervent vigilance to preserve the prevailing bourgeois way of life in North Atlantic societies. . . ."[41]

Instead of defending this liberal commitment, and drawing a sharp line against a radical enemy, Rorty responded with a weak and half-hearted apology: "This fervent vigilance is largely a matter of urging that we hang on to constitutional democracy—the only institutional aspect of the 'prevailing bourgeois way of life' about which I get fervent—while patriotically striving to keep social protest alive."[42] For Rorty, America's constitutional order is only an "aspect" of its existence, without organic relation to (and apparently separable from) its free markets, the institution of private property, and the moral framework of the Judaeo-Christian tradition. Consequently, the radical assault on the foundations of bourgeois society is seen by Rorty as a form of benign surgery.

Note the extravagant self-deception involved in this trope. As a leftist analyzing capitalist societies, Rorty would never think of viewing political institutions as discrete from economic or social conditions. It is only as a revolutionary contemplating the socialist future that he allows himself to disregard these links. In fact, it is only by severing the connection between property and freedom that Rorty can think of himself as a "liberal" and at the same time sympathize with an anti-American radical whose agenda is the destruction of liberal society.

Rorty's posture is that of the classic fellow traveler who wills the ends of revolution but not the means. Starting from a premise of universal skepticism, Rorty concludes by hoping for the victory of believers in a radical faith. He explains his own pragmatism as "a repudiation of the quest for certainty and foundations, which [Cornel] West has described as 'the evasion of philosophy,'" but adds, "This evasion is socially useful only if teamed up with prophecies—fairly concrete prophecies of a utopian social future."[43] In other words, in the real world, the pragmatic Rorty is willing to surrender his epistemological skepticism to the crude zealotry of a Cornel West. The "concrete prophecies" Rorty refers to, of course, are the familiar radical utopias—the egalitarian futures of Rousseau and Marx: "Suppose that somewhere, someday, the newly-elected government of a large industrialized society decreed that everybody would get the same income, regardless of occupation or disability. . . . That country would become an irresistible example. . . . Sooner or later the world would be changed."[44] Indeed it would, as the example of all the Marxist *gulags* attest.

Rorty's wish to be "socially useful" is thus a form of the religious desire that the modern temper denies, and that radical messianism exists to satisfy. It is the desire that creates a popular front between Jacobins and liberals in search of the egalitarian Eden. Nothing could demonstrate more clearly how the abiding root of the revolutionary impulse lies not in the frailty of the human intellect but in the weakness of the human heart.

For radicals, it is not socialism, but only the language of socialism that is finally dead. To be reborn, the Left had only to rename itself in terms that did not carry the memories of insurmountable defeat, to appropriate a past that could still be victorious. This task is already well under way. In the wake of the Communist collapse, radicals have sought to distance themselves from their support for foreign utopias that failed and to revive the Marxist chimera as an American dream: "The grand social narrative of American life," two leftists argued in the *Los Angeles Times* shortly after the fall of the Berlin Wall, "is what we might call the Drama of Democracy: a messianic, at times apocalyptic, struggle to secure a world where all people will be free, equal, independent and without want."[45] In this way, the utopian fantasy that has filled the world with so much suffering and unhappiness in our time is revived as a patriotic, "populist" vision. "The dramatic tension [in America's social narrative]," these radicals write, "arises from the struggle to make this 'American Dream' available to everyone."

But just how the dream is to be made available makes all the difference in the world. If it is by removing the barriers to opportunity, so that individuals can rise as a result of their own efforts, then there will be continuity with the freedoms Americans have enjoyed from the founding to the present. But if the dream is to be delivered by political power, by class-, race-, and gender-warfare, and by the forced redistribution of resources between contending social groups, then the outcome can only be another grim experiment in totalitarian futures. The dramatic tension of the American narrative remains, in fact, what it has always been: a tension between democracy understood as limits to government, the liberal polity of a diverse citizenry, and democracy understood as radicals understand it, the righteousness of a guardian state.

CHAPTER TWO

THE FATE OF THE MARXIST IDEA

PEOPLE WHO IDENTIFY WITH THE LEFT OFTEN ASK THE following question: How is it possible for decent human beings *not* to be progressive like us? How can they not share our concern for social justice or the better world we are attempting to create? The answers offered by progressives are that ignorance clouds the understanding of others and social privilege blocks their human responses. In the eyes of progressives, their conservative opponents are prisoners of a false consciousness that prevents them from recognizing human possibility. This false consciousness is rooted in the self-interest of a ruling class (or gender, or race), which is intent on defending the system that secures its privilege. In other words, opposition to progressive agendas grows naturally from human selfishness, myopia and greed. To progressives, theirs alone is the vocation of reason and compassion.

The Right has questions too: How is it possible for progressives to remain so blind to the grim realities their efforts have produced? How can they overlook the crimes they have committed against the poor and oppressed they set out to defend? How can they have learned so little from the history their ideas have engendered?

Progressives have a false consciousness of their own. Being so noble in their own eyes, how could they *not* be blind? But this blindness also springs from an insularity created by their contempt for those not gifted with progressive sight. As a result, radicals are largely innocent of the ideas and perspectives that oppose their agendas. The works of von Mises, Hayek, Aron, Popper, Oakeshott, Sowell, Strauss, Bloom, Kirk, Kristol and other antisocialist thinkers are virtually unknown on the Left—excluded from the canons of the institutions they dominate and absent from the texts they write. This silencing of ideological opponents in the areas of the culture the Left controls has led to a situation one academic philosopher lamented as "the collapse of serious argument throughout the lower reaches of the humanities and the social sciences in the universities."[1] The same judgment cannot be made about the excluded conservatives who are forced by the cultural dominance of the Left (and by the historic ferocity of the radical assault) to be thoroughly familiar with the intellectual traditions and arguments that sustain it. This is one reason for the vitality of contemporary conservative thought outside the academy from which it has been driven.

Following the collapse of the socialist empire, the marginalization of conservative ideas in the academic culture has been so pervasive that even those conservatives whose analyses were dramatically vindicated by the events continue to remain hopelessly obscure. As far back as 1922, Ludwig von Mises wrote a five-hundred-page treatise predicting that socialism would not work. Socialist theorists, he wrote, had failed to recognize basic economic realities that would eventually bankrupt the future they were creating. These included the indispensability of markets for allocating resources, and of private property for providing the incentives that drive the engines of social wealth. Moreover, socialists showed no inclination to take seriously the problems their schemes created: "Without troubling about the fact that they had not succeeded in disproving the assertion of the liberal school that productivity under socialism would sink so low that want and poverty would be general, socialist writers began to promulgate fantastic assertions about the increase in productivity to be expected under socialism."[2]

As close as any analysis could, von Mises's warning anticipated the next seventy years of socialist history. Under the Soviet Union's central plans, the Kremlin rulers were indeed unable to allocate resources rationally, or to promote technological innovation, or to replace the profit motive with a viable system of non-monetary "social" incentives. As a result, the socialist economy was unable to keep abreast of the technological changes that would catapult the West into the post-industrial era. The socialist economy could not even create sufficient growth to feed its own people. Once the breadbasket of Europe, Soviet Russia under socialist planning became a chronic importer of grain, an economy of forced rationing and periodic famine. The effect of socialist order was exactly as von Mises had predicted—the generalization of poverty and the crippling of productivity, so that Russia was unable to enter the information age and compete economically with the West.

Although history has dramatically confirmed von Mises's analysis, and just as dramatically refuted his left-wing opponents, his intellectual contributions are as unrecognized today as they were before the Communist fall. While the intellectual tradition that gave rise to von Mises's insights is marginalized in American universities, and its paradigm ignored, Marxism and its variants flourish. The profusion of Marxists on university faculties today, is unprecedented, while the theories that Marxism has spawned now provide the principal texts for the next generations. Von Mises's writings are invisible, but the works of Stalinists, ignorant of the most basic economic realities of how modern societies function, are familiar to most undergraduates. In the humanities and social sciences, the discredited tradition of Marxism has become the intellectual wellspring of the main schools of current academic theory—critical studies, cultural studies, historicism, structuralism, postmodernism and radical feminism. The comparable schools of conservative and libertarian thought are hardly extant within university walls.

It is scarcely necessary to add that no serious attempt has been made by progressive intellectuals to revisit von Mises's critique. Or to come up with answers that would justify the respect now accorded to the bankrupt intellectual tradition of the Left, or arguments that would warrant this revived commitment to a discredited faith. Given the verdict of history on the socialist experiments, von Mises's works and others that derive from the tradition of classical liberalism should provide the central texts of any respectable academic discourse. Instead, they are so marginal to the university curriculum, it is as if they had never been written.

In contrast to von Mises's fate, Stalinist intellectuals like Antonio Gramsci have become icons of the left-wing professoriat, their writings reissued in scholarly editions, their texts well thumbed by undergraduates, and their ideas developed and refined in doctoral studies. Despite its dismal record of collusion and failure, the tradition of the Left is intellectually dominant in the American university today in a way that its disciples would never have dreamed possible thirty years ago. As though the human catastrophes produced by its ideas had never taken place.

Von Mises, of course, is not alone. His disciple, Friedrich Hayek—to take another representative example—is equally obscure in the academic culture. The theoretical edifice Hayek created is, like von Mises's, as comprehensive as Marxism, and has been vindicated by the same history that has refuted Marx's ideas. He has even been awarded a Nobel Prize in economics. Yet the name Hayek is all but absent from the discourse of the Left, and from the academic curriculum the Left has designed. Typically, Hayek's mature works on capitalism and socialism are rarely if ever mentioned in the broad intellectual culture, their arguments never confronted. The average college graduate is acquainted with whole libraries of radical blather—the repackaging by third-rate intellects of discredited Marxist formulas in the works of bell hooks, Frederic Jameson, Derrick Bell, Andrew Ross, Richard Delgado and Catharine MacKinnon—but has never opened a text by the most important figures of Twentieth-Century social thought.

An ideological *omertà* is the Left's response to its vindicated critics, especially those who emerged from its own ranks. It is an intellectual version of Stalin's efforts to transform his political opponents into "unpersons," in order to obliterate their influence and ideas. The historian

Aileen Kraditor, once a star in the firmament of the academic Left, is a less prominent intellectual figure than von Mises and Hayek, but no less illustrative of the method by which the Left deals with its critics. The books Kraditor wrote—*The Ideas of the Woman Suffrage Movement, Means and Ends in American Abolitionism* and *The Radical Persuasion*—were once routinely cited by Sixties progressives as models of the scholarship radicals produced. But then Kraditor had second thoughts and departed the radical ranks. As a pioneer in feminist scholarship, Aileen Kraditor would have been a prime candidate for high honors in today's academy. But she had the bad judgment to become an anti-Communist and to write a book puncturing the radical illusion. As a result, it is as though she had never existed, and never written.

Based on her own experience as a member of the Party during the height of the Cold War, Kraditor's last book set out to describe the intellectual worldview of American Communists. *"Jimmy Higgins": The Mental World of the American Rank-and-File Communist, 1930–1958*[3] is the definitive study of its subject. Yet, despite an explosion of academic interest in the history of American Communism, Kraditor's work is almost never referred to and almost never cited, its insights never engaged by the academic community. Instead, Communist sympathizers like Princeton's Ellen Schrecker and NYU's Robin D. G. Kelley, have become preeminent academic authorities on the historiography of American Communism, while Aileen Kraditor has been made an unperson in the intellectual culture.

This politically motivated censorship and self-enforced ignorance insulates the Left from uncomfortable encounters with former comrades and necessary truths. Defectors from the radical ranks quickly discover that their ideas are ignored and their realities erased.[4] It is the way a bankrupt intellectual tradition enforces its academic rule. The unwritten law of the radical intellect is this: once the revolutionary idea has been called into question, the questioner must cease to exist. In a democracy, this extinction may be accomplished by personal smear or ideological exclusion. But it is required in order to preserve the faith. To the religious mind, the thought of God's death is unthinkable.

The two letters that follow were attempts to pursue a dialogue beyond, as it were, the revolutionary grave. They were efforts to distill and communicate the experience of a lifetime to those who remained trapped inside a bankrupt faith. Both attempts failed. The first elicited the threat of a lawsuit; the second was answered by an insult and silence.[5]

I

UNNECESSARY LOSSES

Communism is the philosophy of losers.
—Daniel, *The Book of Daniel*

April 1987

Dear Carol,[6]

I'm sorry it has taken me so long to answer your letter. When I returned to California after my father's funeral, I spent a long time thinking about what happened during that weekend in New York. I thought about my phone call to you on Friday after I came back from the cemetery; how I had invited you to the memorial service we had planned for Sunday at my mother's house; how you had said you would come and how comforting that felt; how our conversation had turned to politics and changed into an argument, and our voices had become angry; how I had begun to feel invisible, and how the loneliness this caused in me became so intense I said we should stop; and how, when we could not stop, I hung up.

I thought about my feelings when you did not call back that day or the next; and when you did not come to my father's memorial on Sunday as you had said you would. I thought about the plane ride back home, when I began to realize how deep the wound in our friendship had become.

I thought about how our friendship had begun nearly half a century before at the Sunnyside Progressive Nursery School—so long in memory that I have no image of a life without it. In the community of the Left, I guess, it is perfectly normal to erase the intimacies of a lifetime over political differences. Yet on the long plane ride home, it caused me great pain to think that I might never hear from you again.

And then, a week after my return, your letter arrived in the mail. You were sorry, you said, about the way our phone call ended. *Because of our common heritage* (you said) *the personal and the political cannot so easily be separated.* Your words reminded me of the "Khrushchev divorces" of 1956—the twenty-year marriages in our parents' generation that ended in disputes between the partners over the "correct" political position to take toward his secret report on the crimes of Stalin. As though a political idea defined their reality.

But then, as though a political idea defined our reality too, your letter suddenly forgot about what had happened between us as friends, and reopened the wound to resume the argument.

Dear David,

I was sorry that your call ended the way it did. It was not my idea to get into a political argument, but apparently you had a need to provoke it. I would have preferred to talk more about personal matters. But because of our common heritage the personal and the political cannot really be separated. And that is why I can't help thinking that the views you now hold are psychological rather than intellectual in origin.

I want to add some things to clarify my position. I still consider myself part of the left, but my views have changed significantly over the years. I haven't been a Stalinist since I visited the Soviet Union in 1957, when I was nineteen. After that, like you, I became part of the New Left. I no longer consider the Soviet Union a model for the socialist future. But after all the garbage has been left behind I do hold certain basic tenets from my old left background. The first is that there are classes and the rich are not on the same side as the rest

of us. They exploit. The second is that I am still a socialist. I still be-
lieve in theory socialism is better than capitalism. If it has not
worked so far, it is because it has not really been tried.

What concerns me about you is that you have lost the compassion
and humanism which motivated our parents to make their original
choice. There can be no other explanation for your support of the
vile policies of Ronald Reagan. Except that you are operating from
an emotional position which surpasses rational thinking. Also, by as-
suming that because you are no longer "left" you must be "right," you
appear to be lacking a capacity to tolerate ambiguity; and the real
world is indeed ambiguous. Why do you feel the need to jump on es-
tablishment bandwagons? I assume they are paying you well for your
efforts.

Your old (one of the oldest) friend,
Carol

The wound in our friendship is really a mirror of the wound that a political faith has inflicted on our lives; the wounds that political lives like
ours have inflicted on our times.

Let me begin with a concession. It is probably correct of you to
blame me for our argument. *Apparently you had a need to provoke it.* I
probably did. I had just buried a father whose politics was the most important passion in his life. Political ideas provided the only truths he considered worth knowing, and the only patrimony he thought worth
giving. When I was seventeen and had political ideas of my own for the
first time, politics made us strangers. The year was 1956. My father and
I were one of the Khrushchev divorces.

We never actually stopped speaking to each other. But the distance
was there just the same. After I had my own children and understood
him better, I learned to avoid the areas where our conflicts flourished. I
was even able to make a "separate peace," accepting him as the father he
was rather than fighting to make him the one I wanted him to be. But he
never was able to make the same peace with me. In all those thirty years
that were left to us after I left home, there was not a day I was not aware

of the line that politics had drawn between us, not a day that I did not feel how *alien* my ideas made me to him.

Emotions of grief and mourning make a perverse chemistry. If I provoked you to attack me on my father's burial day, perhaps I had a need for it: to do battle with the ideas which in ways and at times seemed more important to him than I was; to resume the combat that was his strongest emotional connection to other human beings and to me. Perhaps I thought I could resurrect his ghost in you, one of my oldest and dearest friends, who despite "all the garbage" you have left behind remain true enough to the faith of our fathers to act as his stand-in.

I don't mean to excuse my provocation, but only to remind you of what you forgot in your political passion that evening and in the silence that followed. Me. David. An old friend in need. I had been obliterated by a political idea. I felt like those ideological enemies of the past whom Stalin had made into "unpersons" by erasing the memory of who they had been. Which is what happened to my father at his own memorial that Sunday you did not come.

For nearly fifty years, our parents' little colony of "progressives" had lived in the same ten-block neighborhood of Sunnyside in Queens. And for fifty years, their political faith had set them apart from everyone else. They inhabited Sunnyside like a race of aliens—in the community but never of it; in cultural and psychological exile. They lived in a state of permanent hostility not only to the Sunnyside community, but to every other community that touched them, including America itself.

The only community to which they belonged was one that existed in their minds: the international community of the progressive Idea. Otherwise, they lived as internal exiles waiting for the time when they would be able to go home. "Home," to them, was not a *place* somewhere other than Sunnyside and America; "home" was a *time* in the future when the Sunnyside and America they knew would no longer exist. No compromise with their home ground could put an end to their exile; only a wave of destruction that would sweep away the institutions and traditions of the communities around them, and allow the international community of the progressive Idea to rise up in their place.

To my father and his comrades the fantasy of this future was more important than the reality around them. All the activities of the Sunnyside progressives—the political meetings they attended five and six nights a week, the organizations they formed, the causes they promoted—were solely to serve their revolutionary Idea. The result was that after five decades of social effort, there was not a single footprint to show that they had really lived in our little ten-block neighborhood. When my father's life came to its close, he was buried as a stranger in the community where he had spent his last fifty years.

My father lived the sinister irony that lies at the heart of our common heritage: the very humanity that is the alleged object of its "compassion" is a humanity that it holds in contempt. This irony defined my father's attitude toward the people around him, beginning with those who were closest—the heirs of his Jewish heritage, whose community center he would never be part of and whose synagogue he would never enter. Every Friday night, his own mother still lit the *shabat* candles, but as a progressive he had left such "superstitions" behind. To my father, the traditions his fellow Jews still cherished as the ark of their survival were but a final episode in the woeful history of human bondage, age-old chains of ignorance and oppression from which they would soon be set free. With the members of the real communities around him my father was unable to enjoy the fraternity of equals based on mutual respect.

The only community my father respected was the community of other people who shared his progressive Idea, people like your parents. To my father and his Sunnyside comrades, this meant the orthodoxies that comprised the Stalinist faith. But when he was just past fifty, a Kremlin earthquake shattered the myth that held together the only community to which my father belonged. The year was 1956. It was the year my father's world collapsed.

By the time I reached Sunnyside from California, my mother had already decided that his burial arrangements would be made by the Shea Funeral Home on Skillman Avenue. The Shea Funeral Home had been the last stop for the Catholics of the neighborhood for as long as I could remember. My father hated its very name. To him, the little storefront was a symbolic fortress of the enemy forces in his life—the Christian persecutors of the ghetto past he tried to forget, the anti-Communist crusaders of his ghettoized present. My father took his hate to the grave. But for his widow, the battles were already forgotten, the political passions dead with the past. What was alive was her new solitude and grief, and her terror in the knowledge that everything had changed. To my mother, the Shea Funeral Home was an ark of survival, as familiar and comforting as the neighborhood itself.

My father's burial was attended only by his immediate family. We were accompanied to the cemetery by a rabbi I had somewhat disloyally hired to speak at the graveside after confirming with my mother that she would find his presence comforting too. Having been primed with a few details of my father's life, the rabbi observed that death had come to him the week before Passover, whose rituals commemorated an exodus to freedom not unlike the one that had brought him as an infant from Russia eighty-one years before. Not unlike the dream of a promised future that had shaped his political life.

The place of burial was Beth Moses, a Jewish cemetery on Long Island fifty miles away from Sunnyside, the last of my father's exile homes. It seemed appropriate to me that my father who had struggled so hard in life to escape from his past should find peace in the end in a cemetery called the "House of Moses." And that this final compromise should have been made for him by the international community of his political faith. The grave where my father was buried among strangers was in a section of the cemetery reserved for Jews who had once belonged to the International Workers Order, a long-defunct Communist front that had sold the plots as a fringe benefit to its members.

On Sunday, the last of my father's surviving comrades assembled in my mother's living room for the memorial. No ceremony had been planned, just a gathering of friends. Those present had known my father—some of them for more than fifty years—with the special intimacy of comrades who shared the scars of a common battleground, lifetime cohabitants in a community of exiles.

I could remember meetings when the same room had reverberated with their political arguments in the past. But now that the time had come to speak in my father's memory, they were strangely inarticulate, mute. As though they were unequal to the task before them: to remember my father as a man.

My father was a man of modest achievements. His only real marks were the ones he made on the lives of the individuals he touched. The ones who were there now. The memories of the people who had gathered in my mother's living room were practically the only traces of my father still left on this earth. But when they finally began to speak, what they said was this: *Your father was a man who tried his best to make the world a better place . . . your father was a man who was a teacher to others . . . your father was a man who was socially conscious, progressive . . . who made a contribution.*

And that was all they said. People who had known my father since before I was born, who had been his comrades and intimate friends, could not remember a particular fact about him, could not really remember *him*. All that was memorable to them in the actual life my father had lived—all that was real—were the elements that conformed to their progressive Idea. My father's life was invisible to the only people who had ever been close enough to see who he was.

The obliteration of my father's life at his own memorial is the real meaning of what you call "our common heritage."

Our common heritage. Such a precious evasion. Our parents and their comrades were members of the Communist Party, were they not? Our common heritage was Marxism. Your need for the Orwellian phrase is revealing. It can hardly be for the benefit of an old comrade like me. In fact, its camouflage is for you. "Our common heritage" betrays your need to be insulated from your own reality—the reality of your totalitarian faith.

I'm sure this charge upsets you. In your own mind, the only elements that survive of our heritage are the innocent ones: *I haven't been a Stalinist since I visited the Soviet Union in 1957, when I was nineteen. . . . I no longer consider the Soviet Union a model for the socialist future.* But what leftists who are able to enjoy the privileges of *bourgeois* democracy in the

West think of themselves as Stalinists anymore, or the Soviet Union as a socialist model? Such vulgar convictions are reserved for the revolutionary heroes of the Third World who actually wield the power—the Vietnamese and Cuban and Nicaraguan comrades—to whom you and other left-wing sophisticates pledge your loyalties and support. *They* are Stalinists even if you are not.

It is not an idealistic intention, but a totalitarian *faith* that creates the common bond between revolutionary cynics like Stalin and Fidel, the Sandinista *comandantes,* and progressive believers like yourself.

Totalitarianism is the possession of reality by a political Idea—the Idea of the socialist kingdom of heaven on earth; the redemption of humanity by political force. To radical believers this Idea is so beautiful it is like God Himself. It provides the meaning of a radical life. This is the solution that makes everything possible; the noble end that justifies the regrettable means. Belief in the kingdom of socialist heaven is a faith that can transform vice into virtue, lies into truth, evil into good. In this revolutionary religion, the Way, the Truth, and the Life of salvation lie not with God above, but with men below—ruthless, brutal, venal men—on whom faith confers the power of gods. There is no mystery in the transformation of the socialist paradise into Communist hell: liberation theology is a satanic creed.

Totalitarianism is what my father's funeral and your letter are about.

Totalitarianism is the crushing of ordinary, intractable, human reality by a political Idea.

Your letter indicts me because my ideas have changed. I accept the indictment. But the biggest change in me is not in any new political convictions I may have. It is in the new way I have discovered of looking at things. The biggest change is seeing that reality—concrete, messy, common and complex reality—is more important than any idea. In the years since we were close, I have gained respect for the ordinary experience of others and of myself. It is not a change I wanted to make. It is something that happened to me despite my resistance. But it is a change that has allowed me to learn from what I know. To connect, for example, the little episodes of our progressive heritage (like my father's memorial) with the epic inhumanities that its revolutions inspire. It is because you have not changed that these connections remain invisible to you.

What concerns me about you is that you have lost the compassion and humanism which motivated our parents to make their original choice.

Their original choice. Another Orwellian evasion. Their "original choice" was Communism. Our parents were idolators in the church of a mass murderer named Stalin. They were not moralists, as you suggest, but Marxist-Leninists. For them the Revolution *was* morality (and beauty and truth as well). For them, compassion outside the Revolution was mere *bourgeois* sentimentality. How could you forget this? Compassion is not what inspired our parents' political choices. Nor is compassion what inspired the Left to which you and I both belonged—the *New Left* that forgot the people it liberated in Indochina once their murderers and oppressors were red; that never gave a thought to the Cubans it helped to bury alive in Castro's jails; that is still indifferent to the genocides of Marxist conquest—the fate of the Afghanistans, Cambodias and Tibets.

Compassion is not what motivates the Left, which is oblivious to the human suffering its generations have caused. What motivates the Left is the totalitarian Idea. The Idea that is more important than reality itself. What motivates the Left is the Idea of the future in which everything is changed, everything *transcended*. The future in which the present is already *annihilated*, and its reality no longer exists.

What motivates the Left is an Idea whose true consciousness is this: *Everything deserves to perish.* Everything that is flesh-and-blood humanity is only the disposable past. This is the consciousness that makes mass murderers of well-intentioned humanists and earnest progressives, the Hegelian liberators of the socialist cause.

In the minds of the liberators, it is not really *people* that are buried when they bury their victims. Because it is not really people who stand in their way. Only "agents of past oppressions;" only "enemies of the progressive Idea." Here is an official rationale, from a *Cheka* official of the time of Lenin, for the disposal of 30 million human souls: "We are not carrying out war against individuals. We are exterminating the bourgeoisie as a class. We are not looking for evidence or witnesses to reveal deeds or words against the Soviet power. The first question we ask is—to what class does he belong, what are his origins, upbringing, education or profession? These questions define the fate of the accused. This is the essence of the Red Terror."

The Red Terror is terror in the name of an Idea.

The Red Terror is the terror that "idealistic" Communists (like our parents) and "anti-Stalinist" Leftists (like ourselves) have helped to spread around the world. You and I and our parents were totalitarians in democratic America. The democratic *fact* of America prevented us from committing the atrocities willed by our faith. Impotence was our only innocence. In struggles all over the world, we pledged our support to perpetrators of the totalitarian deed. Our solidarity with them, like the crimes they committed, was justified in the name of the revolutionary Idea. Our capabilities were different from theirs, but our passion was the same.

And yours is still. You might not condone some of the crimes committed by the Vietnamese or Cubans, or the Nicaraguan *comandantes*. But you would not condemn them. Or withhold from their perpetrators your comradely support. Nor, despite all your enlightenment since the time of Stalin, are your thoughts really very different from theirs.

Does it occur to you that you condemn me in exactly the same terms that dissidents are condemned by the present-day guardians of the Soviet state? *There can be no other explanation for your support of the vile policies of Ronald Reagan. Except that you are operating from an emotional position which surpasses rational thinking.* In other words, the only explanation for my anti-Communist convictions is that I am "antisocial" and lacking compassion, or insane.

What kind of revolution do you think you and your radical comrades would bring to the lives of the ordinary people who support the "vile policies of Ronald Reagan" in such overwhelming numbers, people for whom you have so little real sympathy and such obvious contempt? The answer is self-evident: exactly the same kind of revolution that radicals of our "common heritage" have brought to the lives of ordinary people wherever they have seized power. For when the people refuse to believe as they should, it becomes necessary to make them believe by force. It is the unbelieving people who require the "Revolutionary Watch Committees" to keep tabs on their neighborhoods, the *gulags* to dispose of their intractable elements, the censors to keep them in ignorance and the police to keep them afraid. It is the reality of ordinary humanity that necessitates the totalitarian measures; it is the people that require their own suppression for the revolution that is made in their name. To revolutionaries, the Idea of "the people" is more important than the people themselves.

Do you see it yet? The compassionate ideas of our common heritage are really only masks of hostility and contempt. We, the revolutionaries, are enemies of the very people we claim to defend. Our promise of liberation is only the warrant for a new and more terrible oppression.

This is the realization that has changed my politics.

These are not clever thoughts that one day popped into mind, but, as you know (and choose to forget), conclusions I was able to reach only at the end of a long night of pain. Until then, I had shared your conviction that we were all radicals for compassionate reasons, to serve benevolent ends. However perverted those ends might have become in the past, however grotesque the tragedies that occurred, I believed in the revolutionary project itself. I believed in it as the cause of humanity's hope. And I was confident that we could learn from history and be able to avoid its destructive turns. We could create a *new* Left that would be guided by the principles of the revolutionary ideal, that would reject the claims of dictators like Stalin who had perverted the revolutions past.

After 1956, I joined others who shared this dream in the attempts to create a new Left in America, and for nearly twenty years I was part of the efforts to make it a reality. But eventually I realized that our efforts had failed. I gave up my political activities and embarked on a quest to understand what had happened. When it was over, I saw that what we had dreamed in 1956 was not really possible. The problem of the Left did not lie in sociopathic leaders like Stalin or Castro, who had perverted the revolutionary Idea. It was the revolutionary Idea that perverted the Left.

Because you knew me from the very beginning, you were aware of the road I had traveled, the connection between what I had lived through and what I had become. No matter how different the traveler appeared at the end of the journey, you were a witness to who he was. To the reality he had lived. But it is clear now that this reality—*my* reality—is something you no longer want to know. You prefer to erase me instead. It is not unlike the erasure of my father's truth that occurred at his memorial service.

Let me tell you some things you once knew but have tried to forget about the person you accuse now of being unable to cope with real-life complexity, of responding to the loss of one ideological certainty by reflexively embracing its opposite.

The formative experience of my politics was the shattering of the Old Left's illusions by the Khrushchev Report and the events of 1956. You and I were seventeen at the time, now suddenly suspended between a political past that was no longer possible and a future that remained uncertain. Our parents' political faith had been exposed as a monstrous lie, making it impossible for us to be "Left" in the way that they had been. But I did not assume therefore that I had to be "Right." I did swear that I would never be part of another nightmare like theirs. But I didn't want to give up their beautiful Idea. So I joined others in our generation who were setting out to rescue the Idea from the taint of the past, to create a Left that was new.

In the years that followed, I could always be seen in the ranks of this Left, standing alongside my radical comrades. But in all those years there was a part of me that was always alone. I was alone because I never stopped thinking about the ambiguous legacy that we all had inherited. I was alone because it was a legacy that my New Left comrades had already decided to forget.

It was as though the radicals who came to politics in the Sixties wanted to think of themselves as having been born without parents. As though they wanted to obliterate the bad memory of what had happened to their dream when it became reality in the Soviet Union. To them the

Soviet Union was no longer a model for the revolutionary future, but it was also not a warning of the revolutionary fate. It was, in the phrase of the time, "irrelevant." The next generation already knew better.

All during the Sixties, I wrestled with the troubling legacies that my comrades ignored. While others invoked Marx as a political weapon, I studied the four volumes of *Capital* to see "how much of the theory remained viable after the Stalin debacle" (as I explained in the preface to a book I wrote called *The Fate of Midas*). Meanwhile, Marxism had gained a new life. For most New Left radicals who were impatient to "bring the System down," it was Marxism that provided the convenient ax. Even if Marx was wrong, he was right. If Marxism promoted the desired result, what did it matter if the theory was false? But to me it mattered. All the nightmares of the past cried out that it did.

In the mid-Sixties, I moved to London and came under the influence of Isaac Deutscher, an older Marxist who had written panoramic histories of the Russian Revolution and the lives of its protagonists Stalin and Trotsky. For me, Deutscher was the perfect mentor, fully aware of the dark realities of the revolutionary past, but believing still in the revolutionary Idea.

Inspired by my new teacher, I expanded my study of revolutionary history and intensified my search for a solution to the problems of our political inheritance. Before his untimely death in 1967, Deutscher encouraged me to expand one of the essays I had written into a full-length literary effort. When *Empire and Revolution* was completed in 1968, it represented my "solution" to the radical legacy. I had confronted the revolutionary Idea with its failures, and I had established a new basis for confidence in its truth. In Europe, my book joined those of a handful of others that shared its concerns, but in America, *Empire and Revolution* stood all by itself. I don't think you will find another book like it written by an American New Leftist during that entire radical decade. In living with the ambiguities of the radical legacy, in my generation I was virtually unique.

When it was published in America, *Empire and Revolution* made no impression. The willful ignorance of New Left activists had by then become an unshakable faith that had long since ceased to be innocent. Alliances had been struck with totalitarian forces in the Communist bloc; Stalinist rhetoric and Leninist vanguards had become the prevailing radical fashions. Even a New Left founder like Tom Hayden, previously immune to Marxist dogmas, had announced plans to form a new "Communist Party." As though the human catastrophes that had been caused by such instruments had never occurred.

In the face of these developments, I had begun to have doubts as to whether a New Left was possible at all. Whether the very nature of the Left condemned it to endless repetitions of its bloody past. But I deferred my doubts to what I saw at the time as a more pressing issue—America's anti-Communist war in Vietnam. Opposing the war was a moral obligation that in my mind took precedence over all other political tasks. The prospect of the revolution that was the focus of my doubts was a reality remote by comparison. Even though I was uncomfortably allied with "Marxist-Leninists" whom I found politically dangerous and personally repellent, I didn't break ranks. As long as the Vietnam War continued, I accepted the ambiguity of my political position and remained committed to the radical cause.

But then the war came to an end and my doubts could no longer be deferred. The revolutionaries we had supported in Indochina were revealed in victory as conquerors and oppressors: millions were summarily slaughtered; new wars of aggression were launched; the small freedoms that had existed before were quickly extinguished; the poverty of the people increased. In Asia, a new empire expanded as a result of our efforts and, over the peoples of Laos and Cambodia and South Vietnam fell the familiar darkness of a totalitarian night.

The result of our deeds was devastating to all that we in the Left had said and believed. For some of us, this revelation was the beginning of a painful reassessment. But for others there were no second thoughts. For them, the reality in Vietnam finally didn't matter. All that mattered was the revolutionary Idea. It was more important than the reality itself. When they resumed their positions on the field of battle, they recalled "Vietnam" as a radical victory. The "Vietnam" they invoked in their new political slogans was a symbol of their revolutionary Idea: *Vietnam has won, El Salvador will win.* The next generation of the Left had begun. The only condition of its birth was forgetfulness, forgetting what really had happened in Vietnam; erasing the memory of its bloody past.

But even before this history had run its course in Vietnam, the refuge I had reserved for myself all these years in the Left had been cruelly destroyed. The murder of an innocent woman by people whom the New Left had celebrated as revolutionary heroes and whom I had considered my political comrades, finally showed me how blind I had been made by my radical faith.

The murder was committed by the leaders of the Black Panther Party. Throughout the Sixties, I had kept my distance not only from the Panthers but from all the Leninists and their self-appointed vanguards. But, at the same time, I still shared the reasoning that made gangs like the Panthers part of the Left. According to this logic, the Panthers had become "politically aware" as a result of the "struggle" and had left their criminal past behind. By the same reasoning, their crimes were not something shameful, but "prepolitical" rebellions against their oppression as blacks. I accepted this logic for the same reason everyone else did. Because it was the most basic tenet of our radical faith: reality was defined by politics, and could be changed by political ideas.

When the decade was over and the war that had fueled its radical passions had begun to draw to an end, the political apocalypse suddenly receded. Almost overnight, the "revolution" disintegrated. Its energies were exhausted, its organizations in varying stages of dissolution, its agendas quietly shelved. The Panthers survived to embrace the change with a new slogan proclaiming "It's time to put away the gun," and the Leninist posturing too. It was a time for practical community efforts, a time for reality. For me, it seemed a moment to end my long alienation in the Left. In 1973, I began a project with the Panthers to create a Community Learning Center in the heart of the East Oakland ghetto.

In creating the Center, I allowed myself to be persuaded by the Panthers that they did not intend to use the facility as a Panther enclave, but to turn it over to the community as a model of what good intentions could do. And I had persuaded myself that my intentions in working with the Panthers to accomplish this end were truly modest: to help the people in the community it would serve. But looking back afterward, I could see that my intentions were not modest at all. Every aspect of what I did was informed by the revolutionary Idea. That was the bond that connected me to the Panthers in the first place. That was what made what we were going to do resonate with the socialist future. That was what made me so ready to trust intentions I should not have trusted and to forget the violent realities of the Panthers' past. That was what inspired me to ignore the surface betrayals of character that provided warnings to others but were dismissed by me as the legacies of an oppression that radical politics would overcome.

So I raised the necessary funds and bought a church facility in East Oakland to house a school for 150 children. I organized technical support systems and teacher training programs and a variety of community services for the Center, and I found a bookkeeper named Betty Van Patter to keep its accounts.

In the winter of 1974, the Panthers murdered Betty Van Patter and ended my career in the Left. I suspected, and was later told by the Panthers, that they had committed the crime. There were others in the Left who suspected them too, people who knew that Betty was not the only person the Panthers had killed.

The Panthers were (and had always been) a criminal gang exploiting the ghetto. But as a vanguard of the Left, they were a far more dangerous gang than when they had been merely street toughs. Whenever the police accused the Panthers of criminal activity, the Left responded with cries of "racism" and "fascist repression," defending their innocence in the same way the Left in our parents' generation had defended the innocence of Stalin. For the Left, the facts were not what mattered. What mattered was the revolutionary Idea.

It was a familiar pattern: the cynical exploiters of the revolutionary cause; the faithful defenders of the revolutionary name; the "political" silences that erased the truth; the blindness of believers like you and me. The legacy that I had tried so hard to leave by joining the New Left had now become the very center of my life.

———

The summer after Betty was murdered, you and I shared a tragedy of our own. Our friend Ellen Sparer, who had grown up with us in that overrich Sunnyside political soil, was brutally raped and strangled by a black youth in her Englewood, New Jersey, home. We all had been members of the Sunnyside Young Progressives, which we founded when we were twelve years old under the covert auspices of the Communist Party. The premier issue of our *S.Y.P. Reporter* featured an editorial I wrote quoting a Negro Communist poet ("We, as a youth club express our feelings best in the words of the great poetess Beulah Richardson, who said: 'let our wholehearted fight be: peace in a world where there is equality'") and an original poem by Ellen herself, about a Negro named Willie McGee, who had been executed in the South for raping a white woman:

> Did he have a fair trial?
> Did they have any Negroes in the jury?
> Did they have any proof of his guilt?
> NO!
> The only proof they had was that he was a Negro. A NEGRO!

In the years that followed, Ellen had been more faithful than either of us to the heritage we shared (joining the Communist Party *after* the invasion of Czechoslovakia). She was a missionary to the people she considered to be most oppressed, naming her third child Martin after Martin Luther King. As a high school teacher, she was devoted beyond the call of professional duty to black youngsters whose problems others considered difficult if not intractable. ("She had the most intense rescue fantasies of anyone I have ever known," you wrote me after her death). To Ellen, these were not individuals with problems, but victims of a racist system that she was determined to change. She would not let her own children play with toy guns or watch TV cartoons because they were violent, but she took real felons who had committed real crimes with real guns into the bosom of her family, "understanding" their actions and then disregarding the implications because the criminals were disadvantaged and black.

She took them all on as a cause, and was willing to incur risks that others would not, making not only her talents and intellect available but her paycheck and her household as well. In your own words, "she was a sucker for a good sob story," losing over $1,000 by *twice* cosigning a loan for one of her students who conned her. On another occasion, she came close to losing her job when one of her outraged neighbors went to the school principal to complain that Ellen had abetted her daughter's flight from home.

On that fateful summer night, it was one of those troubled students, whom Ellen had taken up as a cause and set out to redeem, who returned to her house to murder her in her bed.

That summer, you and I were able to share a grief over the friend we had lost, but we were never able to share an understanding of why she was dead. In your eyes, Ellen died a victim of circumstance; in mine, she died a martyr to a political faith that had made her blind.

Because of this faith, Ellen's middle-class existence was constantly beset by unsuspected enemies and unseen perils. As a young instructor at Queens College, she helped black militants take over a SEEK program she was employed in that they had targeted as racist. By publicly confirming the charge and personally betraying her professional colleagues, she was able to provide the radicals with the keys to their triumph. But, as you noted, "it also ultimately led to the loss of her job—because once the Black and Puerto-Rican Coalition came into power they did not want any troublemakers around to disturb *their* comfortable sinecures!"

Even though her three children were asleep, Ellen had left her house unguarded. In our dialogues, you managed to find a way around this fact, and everything else you knew about Ellen—including the battles you had had with her over locking her doors after her own house was broken into, and her unwillingness to keep her boyfriend's dog in the house when she was alone: "I guess the fact is that Ellen was not killed by her heroics, naïveté, innocence, trust in human nature . . . or idealism. She had the bad luck to be alone that night . . . and had refused to keep Mel's very vicious German shepherd at the house because the neighborhood kids were always in and out." Well, it was a psychotic neighborhood kid who had been "in and out" who finally killed her. And if Ellen had kept Mel's guard dog that night, she would be alive today.

To me, it is evident that Ellen's house was unguarded not by chance, and certainly not because the neighborhood was safe, but because of a political Idea. An Idea that to Ellen was more important than reality itself. The same Idea was expressed in the choice she had made of a place to live—one of the first integrated neighborhoods in America. To Ellen, Englewood was a social frontier that showed whites could live together with blacks. Over the years, experience had chastened Ellen enough for her to begin to lock her doors and to allow Mel's dog to stay when he stayed over. But, in her heart, locked doors and guard dogs were still symbols of racist fear, of a world divided. The night Ellen was killed, her home was unguarded because of her faith in the progressive Idea. The Idea of the future that progressives like her were going to create: the future when human conflicts would vanish as part of the oppressive past; when there would be "peace in a world where there is equality."

In months previous, incidents of violence had been reported in the neighborhood and rumors had made its inhabitants afraid. As a good soldier of the faith, Ellen would not allow herself to surrender fully to this fear. Her house had been recently broken into and she was alone with her children, but she refused to keep the dog that would have saved her life. On the night she was killed, Ellen's house was left unguarded *because* it was unsafe.

Ellen had no more understanding of the black people who lived in her neighborhood than she did of the black militants whom she had helped to dismiss her or the troubled teenager who finally killed her. Ellen had made all of their causes her own; had befriended them and given them her trust until finally she gave them her life. But Ellen never once really understood who they were. How could she possibly have understood? It was not because of who they were that Ellen had reached out to the black people she had tried to help. It was not because of their re-

ality as individuals. It was because of an Idea she had of them as people who were "oppressed."

The night Ellen was killed, the black people in her neighborhood locked their doors. While Ellen was setting a progressive example, her black neighbors worried among themselves about the recent incidents and talked about them even more ominously than the whites. Ellen's black neighbors knew their fear was not symbolic and what threatened them was not an idea. They had a special reason to worry that a dangerous criminal was stalking their neighborhood, because all his previous victims were black.

———————

In Ellen's fate, I saw a mirror of mine. Our progressive mission had been destructive to others and, finally, destructive to us. It had imbued us with the greatest racism of all—a racism that was *universal,* that never allowed us to see people as they really were, but only as our political prejudices required. With Ellen's death, I had come to the last step in my political journey, which was to give up the progressive Idea—the fantasy of a future that made us so blind.

Why was this Idea so hard to give up? Since 1917, perhaps 100 million people had been killed by socialist revolutionaries in power; the socialisms they created had all resulted in new forms of despotism and social oppression, and an imperialism even more ruthless than those of the past. But the weight of this evidence had failed to convince us. We were able to hold on to our faith by rejecting this experience as a valid test. The ugly socialism of record, we explained to ourselves, was not "really" socialism. It was not our *Idea.* (Listen to yourself: *If it has not worked so far, it is because it has not really been tried. . . . In theory socialism is better than capitalism . . . I still believe. . . .*) If there was any validity to the Idea at all, to give up on it seemed an unthinkable betrayal, like turning one's back on humanity itself.

And so, the last question I came to ask was whether there was any reality to the socialist Idea. In 1973, a conference was held at Oxford University with this very question as its main agenda. The organizer of the conference was a Marxist philosopher who was one of the founders of the European New Left and had traveled a road that ran parallel to my own.

When Eastern Europe's satellites rebelled against their Soviet oppressors in 1956, Leszek Kolakowski was one of their leaders. The rebellions were brutally crushed by the Soviet armies, but he remained until 1968 when Soviet tanks again crossed into Eastern Europe to quell dissident Communists in Prague, and Leszek Kolakowski fought a last-ditch defense of his New Left faith. For his efforts, he was expelled from his Party and driven into exile in the West. When Kolakowski organized the Oxford conference on the socialist Idea, nearly twenty years had passed since he had joined the struggle to create a new dawn in the Communist world. For two decades he had led the efforts to create a "humanistic Marxism" and to liberate socialism from its totalitarian fate. But by the time of the conference, Kolakowski could no longer ignore what his experience had shown. He was ready to admit defeat and give up the attempt to resolve the ambiguities we all had inherited.

The paper Kolakowski read at the conference examined the idea of a classless, unified human community—the progressive goal to which we had dedicated our lives.[7] The catastrophic experience of Marxist societies, he showed, had not been an accident. It was implicit in the socialist Idea. The forces required to impose the radical equality that socialism promised inevitably led to a new *in*equality and a new privileged ruling elite. The socialist unity of mankind we all had dreamed of could only be realized in a totalitarian state.

Kolakowski's arguments had been made before by the critics of socialism in every generation since Marx himself. And, in every generation since, the societies that Marxists created had only served to prove them right. And now they had been proven right in mine. In the light of all I had come to experience and know, Kolakowski's arguments were utterly and tragically correct. But I was still not ready to embrace their conclusions, whose consequences seemed as unthinkable as before. I decided to suspend judgment and take Kolakowski's arguments to my comrades in the Left. I wanted to know how they would respond and whether they had the answers that I did not.

I initiated discussions in radical circles and even organized a seminar to address the question "Is Socialism a Viable Idea?" The reactions I encountered proved personally frustrating, but in the end they were finally instructive. Most radicals, I discovered, did not see the issue as one that was important at all. People whose lives were absorbed in efforts to replace an "unjust" society with one that was better were not interested in whether their efforts might actually make things worse. The few who recognized the gravity of the issue reacted to my questions with suspicion and mistrust. To ask whether the socialist Idea was more than a fantasy was like asking believers about the existence of God.

My search finally ended when I was visited by a British New Leftist who had been one of my earliest mentors. In the days when we were all setting out on our journey, Ralph Miliband had guided me in my first encounters with the troubling legacies of the radical past. After Isaac Deutscher's death in 1967, Miliband was the Marxist whose intellect and integrity I respected most. I had not seen him for more than a decade, but I still read the socialist journal he edited. It was the only socialist publication that had printed Kolakowski's recent ideas.

After we had caught up on the years that had passed, I told him about the crisis I had reached. I recalled the impact of Kolakowski's arguments and the resistance I had met when I confronted other leftists with the issues he raised. I told Miliband it seemed irresponsible for radicals like us to call ourselves "democratic socialists" while Kolakowski's arguments remained unanswered and—even worse—when most of the Left didn't care if his arguments could be answered at all. I didn't see how I could justify a commitment to a political movement with a history like the Left's, which was dedicated to destroying society without a viable plan for what would come next. I was still ready, I said, to oppose injustices wherever I perceived them, but I could not be part of a movement that would not examine its goals.

When I was finished, I waited for an answer. Not an answer to Kolakowski (which I knew by then did not exist), but the answer I had been looking for all along. The one that would say: *David, you are not as alone as you think. The experiences of these years since we all began have indeed shown that the crisis of the socialist Idea is the crisis of the Left itself. If this crisis can't be resolved, if socialism is not a viable future, then our radicalism is really nothing more than a nihilistic passion and the Left a totalitarian force. But there is another possibility. The possibility that answers can be found; that a viable conception of socialism will result; a new agenda for the radical forces and a renewal of the radical hope. Ours may be a small contingent in the radical ranks, but the consequences of failure are too great to give up without trying.*

If my old teacher had answered me like this, perhaps the illusion would have been given new life. But when I was finished, Ralph Miliband said: *David, if those are your priorities, you are no longer a man of the Left.* What my old teacher had told me was that the Left was really a community of faith and that I was no longer part of it.

My conversation with Ralph Miliband occurred sometime in the summer of 1979. I did not then leap to the right side of the political spectrum, but waited another five years before casting a vote for Ronald Reagan and the policies that you consider so "vile." During that time and for twenty-four years previous, I had lived in the teeth of political ambiguity—never free from doubts about the Left, but never feeling I had to resolve my doubts by embracing the views of the opposite side. Your image of me not only denies the meanings of my life, but actually reverses them.

And finally misunderstands them. If I had to label the perspective my experience has given me, I would call it "conservative." And would mean by that respect for the accumulated wisdom of human traditions; regard for the ordinary realities of human lives; distrust of optimism based on human reason; caution in the face of tragedies past. Conservatism is not the other side of the coin of radicalism any more than skepticism is the mirror of faith. I have not exchanged one ideology for another; I have freed myself from the chains of an Idea.

Why was my freedom so hard to win? Why is the Idea so difficult to give up? When I asked myself these questions afterward, I realized that to do so had seemed to me, at the time, like giving up something I could not do without—hope itself. Life without the Idea of the socialist future felt to me like life without meaning. It was then I realized that the reason the Idea is so hard to give up is that a radical faith is like any other faith: it is not a matter of politics but of self.

The moment I gave up my radical beliefs was the moment I had to look at myself for the very first time. At *me*. As I really was—not suspended above everyone else as an avatar of their future salvation, but standing alongside as an equal, as one of *them*. Not one whom History had chosen for its vanguard, but a speck of ordinary human dust. I had to look at the life ahead of me no longer guided and buoyed by a redeeming purpose, no longer justified by a missionary faith. Just a drop in the flow to the common oblivion. Mortal, insignificant, inconceivably small.

Marx was a rabbi after all. The revolutionary Idea is a religious consolation for earthly defeat. For the Jews of our Sunnyside heritage, it is the consolation for internal exile; the comfort and support for marginal life. A passage home. Belief in the Idea is the deception of self that made people like my father and you and me feel real.

Self-deception is what links you to the "common heritage" which is so difficult for those who inhabit it to name. Communism was the center of my father's world, but the word never passed the lips of the comrades who rose to speak at his memorial. A political faith dominated both their lives and his, but the faith finally could not be named. To name it would make their lives too uncomfortably real. In their silence was their truth: What my father and his comrades were finally seeking was not a new reality for the world, but an old illusion for themselves—comfort for their lives of pain.

For my father, it was the pain of a chosen son. My father was the only male child of poor immigrants who could not speak English and who were as fearful of the strange world they had come to as the one they had fled. His own father had failed as a provider, and when my father was still only a child, he realized the family had already placed its fate in his hands. From that time until his death, he felt like a man treading water over his head, with the shore drifting out of sight.

At the age of nineteen, my father found a means to support his parents and a life raft for himself in a job teaching English to other immigrant youngsters at Seward Park High School on the Lower East Side. But he continued to live in his parents' apartment until he was thirty, and his own life remained dangerously adrift. Clarity entered my father's life through the Communist Party and the socialist Idea. The moment he joined the Party, he felt himself touch the shore of a land mass that circled the globe and extended into the future itself. As a soldier in the Party's vanguard and a prophet of its political truth, my father gained wisdom and power beyond his faculty, and finally achieved what his own father had not: his self-esteem as a man.

In the memorials of his comrades, there had been no mention at all of the Party that had given my father so great a gift. It was like a secret they all were keeping from themselves. My father would have wanted them to keep their secret, because he had a secret too. *My father had left the Communist Party more than thirty years before.*

It was only toward the end of his life that my father felt able to tell me this secret, and then in a voice full of emotion and pain, as if it had all not happened so many years past. The event had taken place in 1953, when I was fourteen and my father was approaching fifty (which is my age now). The anti-Communist crusade of the early Cold War was reaching its height, and my father was about to lose the raft that had kept him afloat. For twenty-nine years, he had taught English at the same high school on the Lower East Side, but now a new law had been passed that barred Communists from his lifetime vocation.

In the ordinary business of his life outside politics, my father had remained timid like his father before him, clinging all that time to his very first job. But in the drama of history which he now entered, my father was the tall man his faith had made him. He was ready to stand up to his inquisitors and bear the blows they were about to give him. To defend his Party and its cause, my father was even ready to give up his raft of survival and for the first time to plunge into uncharted seas.

It should have been my father's moment of glory, but instead it became his hour of shame. For "political reasons" the Party decided that my father would not be allowed to make his stand as a man on trial for his political beliefs. Instead, he would have to defend himself as the victim of an "anti-Semitic" campaign. All my father's pride as a man lay in the cause that he had joined, in the fact that he had reached the shores of progressive light and had left his Jewish ghetto behind. Even in the best of circumstances, the lie that the Party now required would have been excruciating for a man of my father's temper. But when the court of history called him to account, there was no place for my father to hide.

When his moment came, my father followed the Party line as he always had done. In his moment of glory, my father colluded in his own public humiliation and was fired as a Communist from his only profession, protesting his rights as a Jew.

When my father was betrayed by the Party he loved, he was forced to look at the truth. The Party was everything to him, but to the Party he was nothing at all. His faith in the Party had not really given him power; it had only made him a political pawn. The secret my father could only reveal to me late in his life was the terrible truth he had seen.

This truth made it impossible for my father ever to go back, but he did not have the strength to go forward. He could not leave (any more than you can leave) the faith that was the center of his life. It was a dilemma my father resolved (as you do) with a strategic retreat. He quietly left the Party that had betrayed him, but he kept his political troth. He was never again active politically, but every day of the thirty years he had left, he loyally read the Communist press and defended the Party line.

All those years, my father kept his secret as though he were protecting a political cause. But in fact, as anyone else could see, all those years my father was keeping his secret to protect himself.

My father's deceit was small. The hurt it caused was only to him and his family. But my father's deceit is a metaphor for all the lies of the political faithful, the self-deceit and deceit of others that have made their cause a blight on our time.

The immediate intent of my father's deceit was to conceal the reality of his political cause—its casual inhumanities, its relentless betrayals. But the real purpose of my father's deception was to avoid the reality that made his faith necessary in the first place, that makes the Idea so hard to give up. The reality my father could not confront was his own.

It is the same with you. When you deny my reality for a political Idea, what you really don't want to confront is your own. *I assume they are paying you well for your efforts.* Can you really think I sold out my faith for money? How can you—who know the price that I had to pay for what I have learned—point such a finger at me? Only if you feel so deprived in your own life that your words really mean this: *I am not being paid well for mine.*

The rich are not on the same side as the rest of us. They exploit. The radical truth (which is your truth still) is the *class war* of the social apocalypse, the war that divides humanity into the "haves," who exploit, and the "have-nots," who are oppressed, into those who are paid well for their efforts and those who are denied, into the just and the unjust, into *their* side and *ours*. The radical truth is the permanent war that observes no truce and respects no law, whose aim is to destroy the only world we know.

This is the "compassionate" cause that makes radicals superior to ordinary humanity and transforms the rest into "class enemies" and unpersons and objects of contempt.

Take a careful look at what you still believe, because it is a mirror of the dark center of the radical heart: not compassion, but resentment— the envious whine of *have not* and *want;* not the longing for justice, but the desire for revenge; not a quest for peace, but a call to arms. It is war that feeds the true radical passions, which are not altruism and love, but nihilism and hate.

———

The farcical surfaces of the political divorces over the Khrushchev Report masked a deeper reality of human pain. Consider what terrors of loneliness inhabit the hearts of people whose humanity must express itself as a political construction. Consider what passions accumulate in such unsatisfied souls.

This is the poisoned well of the radical heart: the displacement of real emotions into political fantasies; the rejection of present communities for a future illusion; the denial of flesh-and-blood human beings for an Idea of humanity that is more important than humanity itself. This is the problem of "our common heritage," as you so delicately name it, and it is our problem as well.

Your old friend and ex-comrade,
David

II

THE ROAD TO NOWHERE

The self-deification of mankind, to which Marxism gave philosophical expression, has ended in the same way as all such attempts, whether individual or collective: it has revealed itself as the farcical aspect of human bondage.

—Leszek Kolakowski

October 1990

Dear Ralph,[8]

It has been over a decade since this silence as durable as an iron curtain descended between us. In these circumstances, I have had to depend on others to learn how you regard me these days: how, at a recent social gathering, you referred to me as "one of the two tragedies of the New Left" (the other being a former Brecht scholar who now publishes guides to the nude beaches of America); how my apostasy has inflicted an emotional wound, as though in changing my political views and leaving the Left I had personally betrayed you.

I understand this. How could it be otherwise for people like us, for whom politics (despite our claim to be social realists) was less a matter of practical decisions than moral choices? We were partisans of a cause that confirmed our humanity, even as it denied humanity to those who opposed us. To leave such ranks was not a simple matter, like abandoning a misconception or admitting a mistake. It was more like accusing one's comrades. Like condemning a life.

Our choice of politics was never a matter of partial commitments. To choose the Left was to define a way of being in the world. (For us, the personal was always political). It was choosing a future in which human beings would finally live as they were meant to live: no longer *self-alienated* and divided, but equal, harmonious and whole.

Grandiose as this project was, it was not something we had invented, but the inspiration for a movement that was coterminous with modernity itself. As you had taught me, the Left was launched at the time of the French Revolution by Gracchus Babeuf and the Conspiracy of the Equals. You had it from Marx: "The revolutionary movement, which began in 1789 . . . and which temporarily succumbed in the Conspiracy of Babeuf, gave rise to the communist idea. . . . This idea . . . constitutes the principle of the modern world" (*The Holy Family*). With a terrible simplicity, the Babouvists pledged themselves to "equality or death," swiftly finding the latter—in a prophetic irony—on the Revolution's own busy guillotine.

The victorious radicals had proclaimed a theology of Reason in which equality of condition was the natural and true order of creation. In their Genesis, the loss of equality was the ultimate source of mankind's suffering and evil, just as the arrogant pride of the primal couple had provoked their Fall in the religious myths now discarded. The ownership of private property became a secular version of Original Sin. Through property, society reimposed on every generation of human innocence the travails of inequality and injustice. Redemption from worldly suffering was possible only through the revolution that would abolish property and open the gates to the socialist Eden—to paradise regained.

The ideas embodied in this theology of liberation became the inspiration for the new political Left, and have remained so ever since. It was half a century later that Marx first articulated the idea of a historical redemption, in the way that became resonant for us:

> Communism is the *positive* abolition of *private property,* of *human self-alienation,* and thus the real *appropriation* of *human* nature through and for man. It is therefore the return of man himself as a *social,* i.e., really human, being. . . .[9]

This was our revolutionary vision. By a historical coup, we would create the conditions for a return to the state of true humanity, whose realization had been blocked by the alienating hierarchies of private property. All the unjust institutions of *class* history that had distorted, divided and oppressed mankind would be abolished and human innocence reborn. In the service of this cause, no burden seemed too onerous, no sacrifice too great. We were the Christopher Columbuses of the human future, the midwives of a new world struggling to emerge from the womb of the old. How could I divorce myself from a mission like this without betraying those whom I had left behind?

Without betraying *you,* my political mentor and closest comrade. We had met in London at the beginning of the Sixties, and you quickly became my guide through the moral wilderness created by the disintegration of the Old Left. I was the scion of Communists, troubled by the crimes the Khrushchev Report had recently unveiled; you had distanced yourself from official Communism, becoming a charter member of the New Left in that spring of 1956. Even as the unmarked graves of Stalin's victims were reopened and their wounds bled afresh, the New Left raised its collective voice to proclaim the continuing truth of its humanitarian dream. Stalinism had died, not socialism. In the moral and political confusion of those years, it was you more than anyone else who helped to restore my radical faith.

To be sure, I was a willing disciple. To abandon the historic project of the Left required a moral stoicism that I lacked. No matter how great the enormities perpetrated in the name of socialism, no matter how terrible the miseries inflicted, the prospect of a world without this idea, and its promise of justice, was unthinkable to me. To turn one's back on socialism would not be like abandoning a misconception or admitting a mistake. It would be like turning one's back on humanity. Like betraying myself.

And so I too refused to give up on this idea that inspired and ennobled us. I joined you and the pioneers of a New Left who had condemned Stalinism and its brutal past and pledged to keep the faith.

We did not ask ourselves then, however, a question that seemed unavoidable to me later: What was the meaning of this refusal to admit our defeat? For thirty years, with only a minority in dissent, the best, most vital and compassionate minds of the Left had hailed the flowering of the progressive state in Soviet Russia. They had made the defense of Soviet "achievements" the *sine qua non* of what it was to be socially conscious and morally correct. Now the Kremlin itself had acknowledged the monstrous crimes of the progressive experiment, confirming the damning accusations of our political adversaries. In the face of such epic criminality and wholesale collusion, what was the urgency of our renewed dedication to goals that had proved so destructive in the first place? Why were the voices of our enemies not more worthy of a hearing in the hour that seemed to vindicate them so completely? Why were we so eager to hurry past the lessons they urged on us, in order to resume our combat again?

Our radical generation was hardly the first (and not the last) to repent and regroup in such careless haste. The cycle of guilt was integral, in fact, to the progress of the Left. It had begun with the radical birth in Eighteenth-Century Paris—that dawn of human fraternity and reason, which also quickly devolved into fratricidal terror and imperial ambition. Which raises these questions: How have the redemptive illusions that inspire the Left been so relentlessly renewed in radical generation after generation, despite the inexorable rebuke of human tragedy that has attended each of its triumphs? How has the Left negotiated these rebirths? What are the consequences?

In the interlude following Stalin's death, when our generation was reviving its political commitments and creating the New Left, we did not stop to ask ourselves such questions. We were all too busy being born. But two decades later, when I had reached the end of my radical journey and had my second thoughts, I was able at last to see how our own modest histories provided the text of an answer.

———————

Meanwhile, you have had no such second thoughts. Even as I write, you and your comrades are engaged in yet another defiant resurrection—the birth of a new generation of the Left, as eager to believe in the fantasy of a new world as we were before. In this *annus mirabilis* of Communist collapse, when the socialist idea is being repudiated throughout the whole expanse of the Soviet empire by the very masses it claimed to liberate, you and your comrades are still finding ways to deny what has happened, and revive the cause.

For you and the prophets of the next Left, apparently, the socialist idea is still capable of an immaculate birth from the bloody conception of the socialist state. You hope to evade the lessons of the revolutionary experiment by writing the phrase "actually existing socialism" across its pages, thus distinguishing the socialism of your faith from the socialism that has failed. The historic bankruptcy of the planned societies created by progressives, a human catastrophe extending across nearly three-quarters of a century and encompassing hundreds of millions of ruined lives, will not be entered in the balance sheet of the Left. This would require of you and your comrades a realistic accounting and agonizing self-appraisal, of which you are not capable. It would irrevocably taint your noble self-image. You prefer, instead, to regard the bankruptcy and the moral debt as accruing to someone else.

There is nothing new in this shell game. It is the same one we, ourselves, engaged in after 1956, when our slogan was "Stalinism is dead; long live socialism!" Today the demonstrations for democracy in the Soviet bloc are ringing down the curtain on the Communist epoch, but you are certain that these events have no relevance to the ideas that inspired them in the first place. Here is the way you recently defended this past:

> Communist regimes, with the notable exception of Yugoslavia after 1948, never made any serious attempt, or indeed any attempt at all, to break the authoritarian mould by which they had been cast at their birth. Conserva-

tive ideologists have a simple explanation of this immobility: its roots are to be found in Marxism. In fact, Marxism has nothing to do with it.[10]

"Actually existing Marxism" is dead; long live Marxism! This is the political formula of the Left, of your Left, today. Veterans of past ideological wars, like yourself, will be crucial in selling this hope to a new generation. The moral weight of this future will be on your shoulders. In reading your words, I could not help thinking how thirty years ago there was an individual who provided the same hope for you, and who since then has become the intellectual model for my own second thoughts. Perhaps you are tempted to bury this connection. For there were not two, but three New Left apostasies that touched you directly, and of these, the defection of Leszek Kolakowski was by far the most painful.[11]

A philosopher of exceptional brilliance and moral courage, Kolakowski had been the intellectual leader of our political generation. Even the titles of his writings—"Responsibility and History," "Towards a Marxist Humanism"—read like stages of our radical rebirth. By 1968 those stages had come to an abrupt conclusion. When the Czechs' attempt to provide Communism with a human face was crushed by Soviet tanks in 1968, Kolakowski abandoned the ranks of the Left. He did more. He fled, unapologetically, to the freedoms of the West, implicitly affirming by his actions that the Cold War did indeed mark a great divide in human affairs, and that the Left was the wrong side.

Kolakowski's apostasy was challenged by E. P. Thompson, then the foremost English New Leftist, in a hundred-page "Open Letter," which you published in the *Socialist Register, 1973*. Written in the form of a plea to Kolakowski to return to the radical fold, the letter began by paying homage to the example he had set for us all, seventeen years before, and which Thompson now claimed as a "debt of solidarity":

What we dissident Communists [of '56] did in Britain . . . was to refuse to enter the well-worn paths of apostasy. I can think of not one who took on the accepted role, in liberal capitalist society, of Public Confessor and Renegade. No-one ran to the press with his revelations about Communist "conspiracy" and no-one wrote elegant essays, in the organs published by the Congress for Cultural Freedom, complaining that God had failed. . . . We refused to disavow "Communism" because Communism was a complex noun which included Leszek Kolakowski.

Here Thompson put his finger on a central reflex of the New Left revival: our refusal to break ranks with our comrades and join the camp of our Cold War opponents; our ability to repudiate the catastrophic outcome of a generation of radical effort without abandoning the radical cause. Not even the crimes of Stalin could break the chain of our loyalties to the revolt against bourgeois society that had been launched at its inception by the Conspiracy of the Equals.

Because Communism was a "complex noun" that included Kolakowski, we were able to preserve our allegiances to an Idea that still included Communism, if only as a deformed precursor of the future to which we all aspired. Because Communism was a complex noun, we refused to concede that Marxism or socialism, both integral elements of the Communist Idea, were themselves condemned by the Stalinist nightmare. Kolakowski provided the bridge across which New Leftists could march, in a popular front with Communists, to carry on a struggle they had begun nobly but soon distorted, and then tragically perverted. Because Kolakowski was himself a complex noun, having spoken out for intellectual honesty and humanist values while he remained a Communist, we could do this without giving up our critical distance or self-respect.

Kolakowski, of course, was not alone. A generation of Kolakowskis had appeared after '56 to incite and inspire us. When you and I met in London in 1963, it occurred to me that if someone as morally serious and intellectually dedicated as you could still devote himself to Marxism and the cause of the Left, despite Stalinism and all that it had engendered, it was possible for me to do so too.

———

There was one question that Thompson had failed to ask, however, which occurred to me only later: when had Communism *not* been a complex noun that included individuals like Kolakowski (and you)? Even in the most grotesque night of the Stalinist abyss, the Communist movement had included the complexity of intellects as subtle and independent as Trotsky and Lukács, Varga and Gramsci, not to mention the fellow-traveling chorus of "progressive" intellectuals who defended Stalinism while proclaiming their humanism from the privileged sanctuaries of the democratic West. Didn't this say something about the futility of such complexity, or its practical irrelevance?

In our minds, of course, the true complexity of the Communist noun went beyond individuals to encompass the nature of reality itself. It was the Hegelian complexity which the idea of the future introduced into the present that ultimately made us so willing to discount the evils of Stalinist rule. This complexity was a creation of our Marxist perspective, which decreed a divorce between appearance and reality: between class history ruled by impersonal forces and revolutionary history ruled by reason; between present reality and the future to come; this vision of the future was the heart of our radical illusion. We had rejected the crude determinism of our Stalinist precursors, but our confidence in the outcome of the historical process allowed us to put our talents on the Communist side of the global conflict, even though "really existing Communism" was an offense to the spirit of the socialism we believed in. In his "Open Letter," Thompson explained the paradox by which we gave our allegiance to an intellectual abstraction and wound up acting as partisans of a reality we disdained:

> In general, our allegiance to Communism was political: it arose from inexorable choices in a partisan world in which neutrality seemed impossible. . . . But our intellectual allegiance was to Marxism. . . . Thus there is a sense in which, even before 1956, our solidarity was given not to Communist states in their existence, but in their potential—not for what they were but for what—given a diminution in the Cold War—they might become.

Our solidarity was given to Communist states *in their potential.* New Leftists like us refused to become anti-Communist cold warriors and offered "critical support" to repulsive Communist regimes because *we believed they would change,* while capitalist regimes we thought *could not.* It was the "humanist potential" of Communist societies, not their totalitarian realities, that claimed our allegiance. By the same reasoning, we were unimpressed by the democratic realities of the capitalist West, because private property rendered them incapable of such liberation. We refused to join the attack on the Communist camp in Cold War battles, no matter how morally justified, because we did not want to aid those seeking to destroy the seeds of the future the Left had sown in Soviet Russia. We were determined to defend what Trotsky had called "the gains of October," the socialist edicts of the Bolshevik Revolution that had abolished private property and paved the way for a better world. It was our recognition of the epoch-making character of these "gains" that defined our radical faith.

By 1973, Kolakowski had rejected this faith and the politics it inspired. Thompson's "Open Letter" was a refusal to accept the rejection. It was an eloquent plea for the continuing vitality of the socialist future and for the Left's enduring mission as the carrier of historical optimism, the idea that humanity could be master of its fate. It was, above all, a rebuke to the leader who had once inspired but now spurned the radicals of '56. "I feel," wrote Thompson, "when I turn over your pages a sense of injury and betrayal."

Kolakowski no longer believed in Communism as a complex noun. He no longer had faith in what he called the "secular eschatology" of the Left, the political passion that sought to fuse "the essence of man with his existence," to assure that the timeless longings of humanity would be "fulfilled in reality."[12] He no longer believed in the reality of the socialist Idea.

The following year, Kolakowski replied to Thompson in an article in *The Socialist Register* called "My Correct Ideas on Everything," which I read in America. Struggling, then, with my own doubts, I was drawn to his arguments, which seemed to promise an exit from the ideological *cul-de-sac* in which I had come to feel trapped. In these passages, he satirized the formulas that ruled our thinking and exposed the web of double standards that transformed them into a self-confirming creed.

As you know, there is no hallmark of left-wing discourse so familiar as the double standard. How many times had we been challenged by our conservative opponents for the "critical" support we gave to totalitarian states where values we claimed to champion—freedom and human rights—were absent, while we made ourselves enemies of the western democracies where they were defended. In the seventy years since the Bolshevik Revolution, perhaps no other question had proved such an obstacle to our efforts to win adherents to the socialist cause.

In his reply, Kolakowski drew attention to three forms of the double standard that Thompson had employed and that were crucial to the arguments of the Left. The first was the invocation of moral standards in judging capitalist regimes, while historical criteria were used to evaluate their socialist counterparts. As a result, capitalist injustice was invariably condemned by the Left under an absolute standard, whereas socialist injustice was routinely accommodated in accord with the relative judgments of a historical perspective. Thus, repellent practices in the socialist bloc were placed in their "proper context" and thereby "understood" as the product of preexisting social and political conditions (i.e., as attempts to cope with intractable legacies of a soon-to-be-discarded past). Comparable capitalist practices were afforded no such alibis.

Second, capitalist and socialist regimes were always assessed under different assumptions about their futures. Capitalist regimes were judged under the assumption that they could not meaningfully improve, while socialist regimes were judged on the opposite assumption that they *would*. Repressions by conservatives like Augusto Pinochet in Chile were never seen in the terms in which their apologists justified them, as necessary preludes to democratic restorations, but condemned instead as unmitigated evils. On the other hand, the far greater and more durable repressions of revolutionary regimes like the dictatorship in Cuba, were invariably minimized as precisely that—necessary (and temporary) stages along the path to a progressive future. Fifteen years after beginning his rule, the dictator Pinochet agreed to restore democracy and to hold a presidential referendum, which he lost.[13] At the same time, and at a point more than twenty years into his own dictatorship, the socialist tyrant Fidel Castro rejected appeals to hold a parallel referendum in Cuba, and went on to become the longest-reigning dictator in the hemisphere.

Finally, in left-wing arguments the negative aspects of existing socialism were always attributed to capitalist influences (survival of the elements of the old society, impact of anti-Communist "encirclement," tyranny of the world market, etc.). The reverse possibility was never considered. Thus, Leftist histories ritualistically invoked Hitler to explain the rise of Stalinism (the necessity of a draconian industrialization to meet the Nazi threat) but never viewed Stalinism as a factor contributing to the rise of Hitler. Yet, beginning with the socialist assault on bourgeois democracy and the forced labor camps (which were a probable inspiration for Auschwitz), Stalinism was a far more palpable influence in shaping German politics in the Thirties than was Nazism in Soviet developments. The "Trotskyite conspiracy with the Mikado and Hitler," the cabal which the infamous show trials claimed to expose, was a Stalinist myth; but the alliance that German Communists formed with the Nazi Party to attack the Social Democrats and destroy the Weimar Republic was an actual Stalinist plot. Without this alliance, the united parties of the Left would have formed a formidable barrier to the Nazis' electoral triumph and Hitler might never have come to power.

The same double standard underlies the Left's failure to understand the Cold War that followed the allied victory. Leftist Cold War histories refuse to concede that the anti-Communist policies of the western powers were a reasonable response to the threat they faced; instead, the threat itself is viewed as a fantasy of anti-Communist paranoia. Soviet militarism and imperialism, including the occupation of Eastern Europe, are dismissed as merely reactive, defensive responses to western containment. But when the same western actions (political containment and military buildup) produce the opposite result—Soviet withdrawal from Eastern Europe and the end of the Cold War—they are said to have had no influence at all. In sum, negative developments in the Soviet bloc are the consequences of counterrevolutionary encirclement; positive developments come from within.

The double standards that inform the arguments of the Left are really expressions of the Left's false consciousness, the reflexes by which the Left defends an identity rooted in its belief in the redemptive power of the socialist idea. *Of course, the revolution cannot be judged by the same standards as the counterrevolution: the first is a project to create a truly human future, the latter only an attempt to preserve an antihuman past.* This is why, no matter how destructive its consequences or how absolutely it fails, the revolution deserves our allegiance; why *anti*-Communism is always a far greater evil than the Communism it opposes. Because revolutionary evil is only a birth pang of the future, whereas the evil of counterrevolution lies in its desire to strangle the birth.

It was this birth in which Kolakowski had finally ceased to believe. The imagined future in whose name all actually existing revolutions had been relieved of their failures and absolved of their crimes, he had concluded, was nothing more than a mistaken idea.

When Kolakowski's reply to Thompson was printed in the *Socialist Register, 1974,* you prefaced its appearance with an editorial note describing it as a "tragic document." At the time, I was in the middle of my own political journey and this judgment was like the first stone in the wall that had begun to separate us. For I already was aware of just how much I agreed with everything Kolakowski had written.

It is clear to me now, in retrospect, that this moment marked the end of my intellectual life in the Left. It occurred during what for me had been a period of unexpected and tragic events. In Vietnam, America had not stayed the course of its imperial mission, as we had said it would, but under pressure from our radical movement had quit the field of battle. Our theory had assured us the capitalist state was controlled by the corporate interests of a ruling class, but events had shown that the American government was responsive to the desires of its ordinary citizens. Closer to home, a friend of mine named Betty Van Patter had been murdered by a vanguard of the Left, while the powers of the state that we had condemned as repressive had been so impotent in reality as to be unable even to indict those responsible. These events, for reasons I need not review here, confronted me with questions that I could not answer, and in the process opened an area of my mind to thoughts that I would previously have found unthinkable.

The shock of these recognitions dissolved the certainties that had previously blocked my political sight. For the first time in my political life, I became inquisitive about what our opponents saw when they saw us. I began to wonder *what if.* What if we had been wrong in this or that instance, and if so, what if *they* had been right? I asked these questions as a kind of experiment at first, but then with systematic determination until they all seemed to be pushing toward a single concern: what if socialism were not possible after all?

While I was engaged with these doubts, Kolakowski published *Main Currents of Marxism,*[14] a comprehensive history of Marxist thought, the worldview we all had spent a lifetime inhabiting. For three volumes and fifteen hundred pages, Kolakowski analyzed the entire corpus of this intellectual tradition. Then, having paid critical homage to an argument that had dominated so much of humanity's fate over the last hundred years (and his own as well), he added a final epilogue that began with these words: "Marxism has been the greatest fantasy of our century." This struck me as the most personally courageous judgment a man with Kolakowski's history could have made.

By the time I read your review of Kolakowski's book,[15] my own doubts had taken me to the perimeter of Kolakowski's position. Consequently, I approached what you had written in a mood of apprehension, even foreboding. For I already knew that this would be our final encounter on my way out of the community of the Left, the last intellectual challenge I would have to meet.

It was appropriate that the final terrain of battle should be Marxism. Thompson had it right, our allegiance *was* to Marxism. Not to this particular thesis or that doctrinal principle, but to the paradigm itself: politics as civil war; history as a drama of social redemption.[16] If we remained in the ranks of the Marxist Left, it was not because we failed to recognize the harsh facts that Marxists had created, but because we did not want to betray the vision that we shared with the creators.

And so the question that would irrevocably come to divide us was not whether Marxists had committed this revolutionary crime, or whether that revolutionary solution had veered off course, but whether the Marxist Idea itself could be held accountable for the revolutions that had been perpetrated in its name. In the end, it was ideas that made us what we were, that had given us the power of perennial rebirth. Movements rose and fell, but the ideas that generated them were immortal. And malleable as well. How easy it had proved in 1956 to discover humanitarian sentiments in Marx's writings and thus distance ourselves from Stalin's crimes; how simple to append the qualifier "democratic" to "socialist," and thus escape responsibility for the bloody tyrannies that socialists had created.

It was on this very point that Kolakowski had thrown down his gauntlet, declaring that Marx's ideas could not be rescued from the human ruins they had created, that "the primordial intention" of Marx's dream was itself "not innocent." History had shown, and analysis confirmed, that there was no reason to expect that socialism could ever become real "except in the cruel form of despotism."[17] The idea of socialism could not be freed from the taint incurred by its actual practice and thus revitalized, as Thompson and the New Left proposed, because it was the idea that had created the despotism in the first place. Marxism, as Kolakowski had announced at the outset of his book, was a vision that "began in Promethean humanism and culminated in the monstrous tyranny of Stalinism."

You understood the gravity of the challenge. The claim that the Promethean project of the Left led directly to the socialist debacle depended on making two historical connections—between Marxism and Leninism, and between Leninism and Stalinism—thus establishing the continuity of the radical fate. You were contemptuous in your response:

> To speak of Stalinism as following naturally and ineluctably from Leninism is unwarranted. However, to speak of Stalinism as "one possible interpretation of Marx's doctrine" is not only unwarranted but false.

A decade has passed since you wrote this. In the East, it is the era of *glasnost;* the silence of the past is broken, the lies exposed. The Soviets themselves now acknowledge the genesis of Stalinism in Lenin. Yet, even if you were still tempted to resist this connection, it would not detain us. For it is the causal link between Marxism and Stalinism that is the real issue, encompassing both.

Stalinism is not a possible interpretation of Marx. What could you have been thinking to have written this statement, and thus to have blotted out so much of the world we know? Forget the Soviet planners and managers who architected the Stalinist empire and found a rationale in Marx's texts for all their actions and social constructions, including the Party dictatorship and the political police, the collectivization and the terror, the show trials and the *gulag*. These, after all, were practical men, accustomed to bending doctrine in the service of real-world agendas. Consider, instead, the movement intellectuals, the "complex nouns" who managed to be Marxists *and* Stalinists through all the practical nightmares of the socialist epoch: Althusser and Brecht, Lukács and Gramsci, Bloch and Hobsbawm and Edward Thompson too. Subtle Hegelians and social progressives, they were all promoters of the Stalinist cancer, devoting their formidable intellects and supple talents to its metastasizing terror. Were they illiterate to consider themselves Marxists *and* Stalinists? Or do you think they were merely corrupt? And what of the tens of thousands of Party intellectuals all over the world who were not so complex, among them Nobel Prize–winning scientists and renowned cultural artists who saw no particular difficulty in assimilating Stalin's *gulag* to Marx's utopia, socialist humanism to the totalitarian state? In obliterating the reality of these intellectual servants of socialist tyranny, you manifest a contempt for them as thinking human beings far greater than that exhibited in the scorn of their most dedicated anti-Communist critics.

Stalinism is not just a *possible* interpretation of Marxism. In the annals of revolutionary movements, it is the prevailing one. Of all the interpretations of Marx's doctrine since the *Communist Manifesto,* it is overwhelmingly the one adhered to by most progressives for the longest time. Maoism, Castroism, Vietnamese Communism, the ideologies of the actually existing Marxist states—*these* Stalinisms are the Marxisms that shaped the history of the epoch just past. This is the truth that leftist intellectuals like you are determined to avoid: the record of the real lives of real human beings, whose task is not just to interpret texts but to move masses and govern them. When Marxism has been put into practice by real historical actors, it has invariably taken a Stalinist form, producing the worst tyrannies and oppressions that mankind has ever known. Is there a reason for this? Given the weight of this history, you should ask rather: *how could there not be?*

What persuaded us to believe that socialism, having begun everywhere so badly, should possess the power to reform itself into something better? To be something other than it has been? To pass through the *inferno* of its Stalinist tragedies to become the *paradiso* of our imaginations?

For we did believe in such a transformation. We were confident that the socialized foundations of Soviet society would eventually assert themselves, producing a self-reform of the Soviet tyranny. This was our New Left version of the faith we inherited. This refusal to accept history's verdict made socialism a reality still. In the Sixties, when the booming capitalist societies of the West made radical prospects seem impossibly remote, we had a saying among us that the first socialist revolution was going to take place in the Soviet Union.

The lineage of these ideas could be traced back to our original "complex noun": Trotsky, the legend of the revolution who had defied Stalin's tyranny in the name of the revolution. While the Father of the Peoples slaughtered millions in the 1930s, Trotsky waited in his Mexican exile for Russia's proletariat to rise up and restore the revolution to its rightful path. But as the waves of the opposition disappeared into the *gulag*, and this prospect became impossibly remote, even Trotsky began to waver in his faith. By the eve of the Second World War, Trotsky's despair had grown to such insupportable dimensions that he made a final wager with himself. The conflict the world had just entered would be a test for the socialist faith. If the great war did not lead to a new revolution, socialists would be compelled, finally, to concede their defeat, to admit that "the present USSR was the precursor of a new and universal system of exploitation," and that the socialist program had "petered out as a Utopia."[18] Trotsky did not survive to see the Cold War and the unraveling of his Marxist dreams. In 1940, his dilemma was resolved when one of Stalin's agents gained entrance to the fortress of his exile in Mexico and buried an ice pick in his head.

But the fantasy survived. In 1953, Stalin died and a New Left generation convinced itself that the long-awaited metamorphosis was at last taking place. With Stalin's death came the Khrushchev thaw, the famous speech lifting the veil on the bloody past, and a relaxation of the Stalinist terror. To those on the Left who had refused to give up, these were signs that the totalitarian caterpillar, having lodged itself in the cocoon of backwardness, was about to become the socialist butterfly of which they had dreamed.

We had our own "complex noun" to explain the transformation. Our mutual friend, Isaac Deutscher, had emerged from the prewar battles over Trotskyism to become the foremost interpreter of the Russian Revolution to our radical generation. What made Deutscher's analysis so crucial to the self-understanding behind our revival was that he recognized the fact that Stalinism, in all its repugnance, was Marxist reality and had to be accepted as such. You too accepted this then, though it has become convenient for you to deny it now, just as you embraced the Leninist version of Marx's doctrine as the only socialist outlook that had actually produced a revolution. There were social-democratic Marxists, of course, who opposed Lenin and Stalin from the beginning. But you dismissed them as sentimentalists, "socialists of the hearth" you called them, reformers who were content to tinker with capitalism and lacked the fortitude to make a revolution.

Deutscher began with the reality that was given to us: the fact of Stalinism, as it had taken root in the Empire of the Czars. But instead of despairing like his mentor Trotsky, Deutscher began to explain why Stalinism, in spite of itself, was being transformed into socialism. In Trotsky's own theories, Deutscher had found an answer to Trotsky's pessimism. While Trotsky worried that there would be no revolution from below, Deutscher explained to us why it was coming from above.

Stalinism, Deutscher wrote, was "an amalgamation of Marxism with the semi-barbarous and quite barbarous traditions and the primitive magic of an essentially pre-industrial . . . society." In short, Stalinism was the fulfillment of Lenin's famous prescription: *with barbarism we will drive barbarism out of Russia:*

Under Stalinism . . . Russia rose to the position of the world's second industrial power. By fostering Russia's industrialization and modernization
Stalinism had with its own hands uprooted itself and prepared its "wither-
ing away."[19]

We will leave aside, for a moment, the unfounded optimism of this
description of Stalinist economic development, looking only at the theoretical perspective it made possible. In Deutscher's view, the backwardness of Russian society had provided the Bolsheviks not only with a
revolutionary opportunity, but also a historical advantage. They could
avail themselves of modern technologies and social theories. Instead of
relying on the anarchic impulses of capitalist investment, they could employ the superior methods of socialist planning. The result of these in-
puts would be a modern economy more efficient and productive than
those of their capitalist competitors.

According to Deutscher, in mid-century the socialist bloc, which had
hitherto provided such grief for radicals like us, was poised for a great
leap forward:

> With public ownership of the means of production firmly established, with
> the consolidation and expansion of planned economy, and—last but not
> least—with the traditions of a socialist revolution alive in the minds of its
> people, the Soviet Union breaks with Stalinism in order to resume its ad-
> vance towards equality and socialist democracy.

The ultimate basis of this transformation was the superior efficiency of
socialist planning:

> . . . superior efficiency necessarily translates itself, albeit with a delay, into
> higher standards of living. These should lead to the softening of social ten-
> sions, the weakening of antagonisms between bureaucracy and workers, and
> workers and peasants, to the further lessening of terror, and to the further
> growth of civil liberties.[20]

Deutscher wrote these words in 1957, a year in which the Soviets celebrated the fortieth anniversary of the revolution by launching the first

space satellite into orbit. The feat dramatized the progress that had been achieved in a single generation and heralded the end of the Soviets' technological "apprenticeship" to the West. The message of Sputnik to the faithful all over the world, Deutscher predicted, was "that things may be very different for them in the second half of the century from what they were in the first." For forty years, their cause had been "discredited . . . by the poverty, backwardness, and oppressiveness of the first workers' state." But that epoch was now coming to an end. With the industrial leap heralded by Sputnik, they might look forward to a time when the appeal of Communism would be "as much enhanced by Soviet wealth and technological progress as the attraction of bourgeois democracy has in our days been enhanced by the fact that it has behind it the vast resources of the United States."[21]

This was the vision of the socialist future that the Soviet leadership itself promoted. In 1961, Khrushchev boasted that the socialist economy would "bury" its capitalist competitors and that by 1980 the Soviet Union would overtake the United States in economic output and enter the stage of "full communism," a society of true abundance whose principle of distribution would be "from each according to his ability to each according to his needs."

As New Leftists, we took Khrushchev's boast with a grain of salt. The Soviet Union was still a long way from its Marxist goals. Moreover, as Deutscher had warned, any future Soviet progress might be "complicated, blurred, or periodically halted by the inertia of Stalinism, by war panics, and, more basically, by the circumstance that the Soviet Union still remains in a position of overall economic inferiority vis-à-vis its American antipode."[22] Actual socialism was still a myth that Stalinism had created. But it had a redeeming dimension: the myth had helped "to reconcile the Soviet masses to the miseries of the Stalin era," and Stalinist ideology had helped "to discipline morally both the masses and the ruling group for the almost inhuman efforts which assured the Soviet Union's spectacular rise from backwardness and poverty to industrial power and greatness."[23]

Because it seemed credible, Deutscher's sober assessment was for us intoxicating. Its mix of optimism and "realism" became the foundation of our political revival. The turn Marxism had taken in 1917, creating a socialist economy within a totalitarian state, posed a seemingly insoluble riddle. How could socialist progress be reconciled with such a stark retreat into social darkness? What did this portend for Marx's insight that the mode of production determined the architecture of social relations? Building on Trotsky's prior analysis, Deutscher pointed to a way out of the dilemma that would preserve our radical faith.

And no doubt that is why, thirty years later, even as the tremors of *glasnost* and *perestroika* were unhinging the empire that Communists had built, you returned to Deutscher's prophecy as a revolutionary premise. "Much that is happening in the Soviet Union [you wrote in the *Socialist Register, 1988*] constitutes a remarkable vindication of [Deutscher's] confidence that powerful forces for progressive change would eventually break through seemingly impenetrable barriers."[24]

Nothing could reveal more clearly how blind your faith has made you. To describe the collapse of the Soviet Empire as a vindication of Deutscher's prophecies (and thus the Marxist tradition) is to turn history on its head. We are indeed witnessing a form of "revolution from above," but it is a revolution that refutes both Deutscher and Marx. The events of the past years are not a triumph for socialism, but its death knell. The rejection of a planned economy by the leaders of actually existing socialist society, the pathetic search for the elements of a rule of law (following the relentless crusades against "bourgeois rights"), the humiliating admission that the military superpower is in all other respects a Third World nation, the incapacity of the socialist mode of production to enter the technological future and the unseemly begging for the advanced technology that it has stolen for decades from the capitalist West—all this adds up to a declaration of socialism's utter bankruptcy and historic defeat. This bankruptcy is not only moral and political, as we all recognized before, but economic as well.

It is precisely the economic dimension of this bankruptcy that

Deutscher did not foresee, and that forecloses any possibility of a socialist revival. For all of these post-Khrushchev decades, that revival has been
premised on the belief in the superiority of socialist *economics*. This is
the meaning of the claim, so often repeated in leftist quarters, that the
"economic rights" and "substantive freedoms" of socialist states took
precedence over the *political* rights and (merely) *procedural* freedoms
guaranteed by the capitalist West. Faith in the socialist future had come
to rest on the assumption that abundance would eventually flow from the
cornucopia of socialist planning and that economic prosperity would
then lead to political deliverance, the Deutscherian thesis.

In our New Left fantasies, the political nightmare of the socialist past
was to be redeemed by the *deus ex machina* of socialist plenty. The economic bankruptcy of the Soviet bloc buries this faith and brings to an
end the socialist era in human history.

This is the reality you have not begun to face.

———————

It is important to understand this reality, which signals the close of an
historical era. But this can be accomplished only if we do not deny the
history we have lived. You can begin this retrieval of memory by recalling
your critique of Kolakowski ten years ago, which set down the terms of
your defense of the cause to which we were all so committed.

Your complaint against Kolakowski, you remember, was that in de-
molishing the edifice of Marxist theory he had slighted the motives of
those who embraced it and thus failed to explain its ultimate appeal. Kolakowski had portrayed Marxism as the secular version of a religious
quest that went back to the beginning of human history: how to reconcile contingent human existence to an essence from which it was estranged, how to return humanity to its "true self."[25] As Kolakowski
viewed it, Marxism was the messianic faith of a postreligious world. Naturally, such an explanation would be insulting to you. You rejected it as
"superficial," inadequate (you said) to explain Marxism's attraction to "so
many gifted people." In your view, Marxism's appeal was not to those
hungry for religious answers, but to people who responded to the call "to

oppose great evils and to create conditions for a different kind of world, from which such evils would be banished." The call to fight these evils was the crucial factor in enlisting people in the cause of the Left, and you named them: "exploitation, poverty and crisis, war and the threat of war, imperialism and fascism, the crimes of the ruling classes."[26]

Let us pass for a moment over the most dramatic of these evils—exploitation, crisis, war, imperialism, fascism, and the crimes of "ruling classes," including the vast privileges of the *nomenklatura*—from which you will agree Marxist societies themselves have not been free since their creation. Let us consider, rather, the simple poverty of ordinary people, whose redress was the most fundamental premise of the revolutionary plan. Let us look at what has been revealed by *glasnost* about the quality of the ordinary lives of ordinary people after seventy years of socialist effort—not forgetting that 20 million human beings (the figure is from current Soviet sources) were eliminated to make possible this revolutionary achievement.

Official Soviet statistics released during *glasnost* indicate that following seventy years of socialist development 40 percent of the Soviet population and 79 percent of its older citizens live in poverty.[27] Of course, judged by the standards of "exploitative" capitalist systems, the *entire* Soviet people live in a state of poverty.

Thus, the Soviet Union's per capita income is estimated by Soviet economists as about one-seventh that of the United States, more or less on a par with Communist China.[28] In the Soviet Union in 1989, there was rationing of meat and sugar, *in peacetime.* The rations revealed that the average intake of red meat for a Soviet citizen was *half* of what it had been for a subject of the czar in 1913. At the same time, a vast supermarket of fruits, vegetables and household goods, available to the most humble inhabitant of a capitalist economy, was permanently out of reach for the people of the socialist state. Indeed, one of the principal demands of a Siberian miners' strike in 1989 was for an item as mundane and basic to a sense of personal well-being as a bar of soap. In a land of expansive virgin forests, there was a toilet paper shortage. In an industrial country with one of the harshest and coldest climates in the world, two-thirds of the house-holds had no hot water, and a third had no running water at all. Not only was the construction of housing notoriously shabby, but space was so scarce, according to the government paper *Izvestia,* that a typical working-class family of four was forced to live for eight years in a single eight-by-eight-foot room, before marginally better accommodation was available. The housing shortage was so acute that at all times 17 percent of Soviet families had to be physically separated for want of adequate space.

After sixty years of socialist industrialization, the Soviet Union's per capita output of nonmilitary goods and services placed it somewhere be-tween fiftieth and sixtieth among the nations of the world. More manu-factured goods were exported annually by Taiwan, Hong Kong, South Korea or Switzerland, while blacks in apartheid South Africa owned more cars per capita than did citizens of the socialist state. The only area of consumption in which the Soviets excelled was the ingestion of hard liquor. In this, they led the world by a wide margin, consuming 17.4 liters of pure alcohol or 43.5 liters of vodka per person per year, which was five times what their forebears had consumed in the days of the czar. At the same time, the average welfare mother in the United States re-ceived more income in a month than the average Soviet worker could earn in a year.

Nor was the general deprivation confined to private households and individuals. The public sector was equally desolate. In the name of progress, the Soviets had devastated the environment to a degree un-known in other industrial states. More than 70 percent of the Soviet at-mosphere was polluted with five times the permissible limit of toxic chemicals, and thousands of square miles of the Soviet land mass was poi-soned by radiation. Thirty percent of all Soviet foods contained haz-ardous pesticides, and 6 million acres of productive farmland were lost to erosion. More than 130 nuclear explosions had been detonated in Euro-pean Russia for geophysical investigations to create underground pres-sure in oil and gas fields, or just to move earth for building dams. The Aral Sea, the world's largest inland body of water, was dried up as the result of a misguided plan to irrigate a desert. Soviet industry operated under no controls, and the accidental spillage of oil into the country's ecosystems took place at the rate of nearly a million barrels a day.[29]

Even in traditional areas of socialist concern, the results were catastrophic. Soviet spending on health was the lowest of any developed nation, and basic health conditions were on a level with those in the poorest of Third World countries. Thirty percent of Soviet hospitals had no running water, the training of medical personnel was poor, equipment was primitive and medical supplies scarce. (By way of comparison, U.S. expenditures on medical technology alone were twice as much as the entire Soviet health budget.) The bribery of doctors and nurses to get decent medical attention and even amenities like blankets in Soviet hospitals was not only common, but routine. So backward was Soviet medical care, thirty years after the launching of Sputnik, that 40 percent of the Soviet Union's pharmacological drugs had to be imported, and much of these were lost to spoilage due to primitive and inadequate storage facilities. Bad as these conditions were generally, in the ethnic republics they were even worse. In Turkmenistan, fully two-thirds of the hospitals had no indoor plumbing. In Uzbekistan, 50 percent of the villages were reported to have no running water and 93 percent no sewers. In socialist Tajikistan, according to a report in *Izvestia*, only 25 to 30 percent of the schoolchildren were found to be healthy. As a result of bad living conditions and inadequate medical care, life expectancy for males throughout the Soviet Union was twelve years less than for males in Japan and nine years less than in the United States, and less for Soviet males themselves than it had been in 1939.

Educational conditions were no less extreme. "For the country as a whole," according to one Soviet report, "21 percent of pupils are trained at school buildings without central heating, 30 percent without water piping and 40 percent lacking sewerage."[30] In other words, despite subzero temperatures, the socialist state was able to provide schools with only outhouse facilities for nearly half its children. Even at this impoverished level, only nine years of secondary schooling were provided on average, compared to twelve years in the United States, while only 15 percent of

Soviet youth were able to attend institutions of higher learning, compared to 34 percent in the U.S.

In Deutscher's schema, Soviet schools ("the world's most extensive and modern education system," as he described it) were the keys to its progressive project. But, as *glasnost* revealed, Soviet spending on education had declined in the years since Sputnik (while U.S. spending tripled). By the 1980s, it was evident that education was no more exempt from the generalized poverty of socialist society than other nonmilitary fields of enterprise. Seduced by Soviet advances in nuclear arms and military showpieces like Sputnik, Deutscher labored under the illusion of generations of the Left. He too believed that the goal of revolutionary power was something other than power itself.

For years the Left had decried the collusion between corporate and military interests in the capitalist West. But all that time the *entire* socialist economy was little more than one giant military-industrial complex. Military investment absorbed 25 percent of the Soviet gross product (compared to only 6 percent in the United States), and military technology provided the only product competitive for export. Outside the military sector, as *glasnost* revealed, the vaunted Soviet industrial achievement was little more than a socialist mirage, imitative, archaic, inefficient and one-sided. It was presided over by a sclerotic *nomenklatura* of state planners, incapable of adjusting to dynamic technological change. In the Thirties, the political architects of the Soviet economy had overbuilt a heavy industrial base, and then, as if programmed by some invisible bureaucratic hand, had rebuilt it again and again.

Straitjacketed by its central plan, the socialist world was unable to enter the "second industrial revolution" that began to unfold in countries outside the Soviet bloc after 1945. By the beginning of the 1980s, the Japanese already had thirteen times the number of large computers per capita as the Soviets and nearly sixty times the number of industrial robots (the U.S., on the other hand, had three times the computer power of the Japanese). "We were among the last to understand that in the age of information sciences the most valuable asset is knowledge, springing from human imagination and creativity," complained Soviet President

Gorbachev in 1989. "We will be paying for our mistake for many years to come."[31] While capitalist nations, including recent Third World economies like South Korea, were soaring into the technological future, Russia and its satellites were caught in the contradictions of an archaic mode of production and stagnating in a decade of zero growth, becoming what one analyst described as "a gigantic Soviet socialist rust belt."[32] In the 1980s, the Soviet Union had become a military superpower, but the achievement bankrupted its already impoverished society in the process.

Nothing illustrated this bankruptcy more poignantly than the opening of a McDonald's fast-food outlet in Moscow about the time the East Germans were tearing down the Berlin Wall. In fact, the semiotics of the two were inseparable. During the last decades of the Cold War, the Wall had come to symbolize the borders of the socialist world, the Iron Curtain that held its populations captive against the irrepressible fact of the superiority of the capitalist societies in the West. When the Wall was breached, the terror was over, and with it the only authority ever really commanded by the socialist state.

The appearance of the Moscow McDonald's revealed the prosaic truth that lay behind the creation of the Wall and the bloody epoch that it had come to symbolize. Its Soviet customers gathered in lines exceeding in length those of the idolators waiting outside Lenin's tomb, the altar of the revolution itself. Here the capitalist genius for catering to the ordinary desires of ordinary people was spectacularly displayed, along with socialism's systemic lack of concern for the needs of common humanity. McDonald's executives even found it necessary to purchase and manage their own special farm in Russia, because Soviet potatoes, the very staple of the people's diet, were too poor in quality and unreliable in supply. On the other hand, the wages of the Soviet customers were so depressed that a hamburger and fries was equivalent in rubles to half a day's pay. And yet this most ordinary of pleasures—the bottom of the food chain in the capitalist West—was still such a luxury for Soviet consumers that to them it was worth a four-hour wait and four hours' wages.

Of all the symbols of the epoch-making year, this McDonald fest was perhaps the most resonant for leftists of our generation. Impervious to the way the unobstructed market democratizes wealth, the New Left had focused its social scorn precisely on those plebeian achievements of consumer capitalism that brought services and goods efficiently and cheaply to ordinary people. Perhaps the main theoretical contribution of our generation of New Left Marxists was an elaborate literature of cultural criticism made up of sneering commentaries on the "commodity fetishism" of bourgeois cultures and the "one-dimensional" humanity that commerce produced. The function of such critiques was to make its authors superior to the ordinary liberations of societies governed by the principles of consumer sovereignty and market economy. For New Leftists, the leviathans of postindustrial alienation and oppression were precisely these "consumption-oriented" corporations, like McDonald's,[33] that offered inexpensive services and goods to the working masses—some, like the Sizzler restaurants, in the form of "all you can eat" menus that embraced a variety of meats, vegetables, fruits and pastries virtually unknown in the Soviet bloc.

These mundane symbols of consumer capitalism revealed the real secret of the era that was now ending, the reason why the Iron Curtain and its Berlin Walls were necessary, why the Cold War itself was an inevitable by-product of socialist rule: in 1989, for two hours' labor at the minimum wage, an American worker could obtain, at a corner Sizzler, a feast more opulent, more nutritionally rich and gastronomically diverse than anything available to almost all the citizens of the socialist world (including the elite) at almost any price.

———————

In the counterrevolutionary year 1989, on the anniversary of the Bolshevik Revolution, a group of protesters raised a banner in Red Square that summed up an epoch: Seventy Years On The Road To Nowhere. They had lived the socialist future and it didn't work.

This epic of human futility reached a climax the same year, when the socialist state formally decided to return the land it had taken from its peasants half a century before. The collectivization of agriculture in the

Thirties had been the very first pillar of the socialist Plan and one of the bloodiest episodes of the revolutionary era. Armies were dispatched to the countryside to confiscate the property of its recalcitrant owners, conduct mass deportations to the Siberian *gulag,* liquidate the kulaks and herd the survivors into the collective farms of the Marxist future.

In this "final" class struggle, no method was considered too ruthless to midwife the new world from the old. "We are opposed by everything that has outlived the time set for it by history," wrote Maxim Gorky. "This gives us the right to consider ourselves again in a state of civil war. The conclusion naturally follows that if the enemy does not surrender, he must be destroyed." The destruction of the class enemy—the most numerous and productive element of Soviet society at the time—was accomplished by massacres, by slow deaths in concentration camps and deliberately induced genocidal famine. In the end, over 10 million people were killed, more than had died on all sides in World War I.[34]

But the new serfdom the Soviet rulers imposed in the name of liberation only destroyed the peasants' freedom and incentive, and thus laid the foundations of the final impasse. Before collectivization, Russia had been the "breadbasket of Europe," supplying 40 percent of the world's wheat exports in the bumper years 1909 and 1910.[35] But socialism ended Russia's agrarian plenty and created permanent deficits—not merely the human deficit of those who perished because of Stalinist brutalities during the collectivization, but a deficit in grain that would never be brought to harvest because of the brutality inherent in the socialist idea. Half a century after the socialist future had been brought to the countryside, the Soviet Union had become a net *importer* of grain, unable to produce enough food to feed its own population.

These deficits eventually forced the state to allow a portion of the crop to be sold on the suppressed private market. Soon, 25 percent of Soviet grain was being produced on the 3 percent of the arable land reserved for private production. Thus, necessity had compelled the Soviet rulers to create a dramatic advertisement for the system they despised. They had rejected the productive efficiencies of the capitalist system as exploitative and oppressive. Yet, the socialist redistribution of wealth had produced neither equity nor justice, but scarcity and waste instead. At the end of the 1980s, amid growing general crisis, Soviet youth were using bread as makeshift footballs because its price had been made so artificially low that it was now less than the cost of the grain used to produce it. This was a microcosm of socialist economy. Irrational prices, bureaucratic chaos, and generalized public cynicism (the actually existing socialist ethos in all Marxist states) had created an environment in which 40 percent of the food crop was lost to spoilage before ever reaching the consumer. And so, half a century after 10 million people had been sacrificed to "socialize the countryside," those who had expropriated the land were ready to give it back.

The road to nowhere had become a detour. *(Soviet joke: What is socialism? The longest road from capitalism to capitalism.)* Now the Soviet rulers themselves had begun to say that it had all been a horrible "mistake." Socialism did not work. Not even for them.

Of all the scenarios of the Communist *Götterdämmerung,* this denouement had been predicted by no one. Ruling classes invariably held fast to the levers of their power. They did not confess their own bankruptcy and then proceed to dismantle the social systems that sustained their rule, as this one had. The reason for the anomaly was this: the creators and rulers of the Soviet Union had indeed made a mistake. The system did not work, not even in terms of sustaining the power of its ruling class.

The close of the Soviet drama was unpredicted because the very nature of the Soviet Union was without precedent. It was not an organic development, but an artificial creation, the first society in history to be dreamed up by intellectuals and constructed according to plan. The crisis of Soviet society was not so much a traditional crisis of legitimacy and rule, as it was the crisis of an *idea,* a monstrously wrong idea that had been imposed on society by an intellectual elite; an Idea so passionately believed and yet so profoundly mistaken, that it had caused more human misery and suffering than any single force in history before.

This suffering could not be justified by the arguments of the Left that the revolutionary changes were "at least an improvement on what existed before." Contrary to the progressive myth that radicals invented to justify their failures, czarist Russia was not a merely pitiful, semibarbaric state when the socialists seized power. By 1917, Russia was already the fourth industrial power in the world. Its rail networks had tripled since 1890, and its industrial output had increased by three-quarters since the century began. Over half of all Russian children between eight and eleven years of age were enrolled in schools, while 68 percent of all military conscripts had been tested literate. A cultural renaissance was underway in dance, painting, literature and music, the names Blok, Kandinsky, Mayakovsky, Pasternak, Diaghelev, Stravinsky were already figures of world renown. In 1905, a constitutional monarchy with an elected parliament had been created, in which freedom of the press, assembly and association were guaranteed, if not always observed. By 1917, legislation to create a welfare state, including the right to strike and provisions for workers' insurance, was already in force and, before it was dissolved by Lenin's Bolsheviks, Russia's first truly democratic parliament had been convened.[36]

The Marxist Revolution destroyed this achievement, tearing the Russian people out of history's womb and robbing whole generations of their minimal birthright, the opportunity for a decent life. Yet even as this political abortion was being completed and the nation was plunging into its deepest abyss, the very logic of revolution forced its leaders to expand their Lie: to insist that the very nightmare they had created was indeed the kingdom of freedom and justice the revolution had promised.

It is in this bottomless chasm between reality and promise that our own argument is finally joined. You seek to separate the terror-filled actualities of the Soviet experience from the magnificent harmonies of the socialist dream. But it is the dream itself that begets the reality, and requires the terror. This is the revolutionary paradox you want to ignore.

Isaac Deutscher had actually appreciated this revolutionary equation, but without ever comprehending its terrible finality. The second volume of his biography of Trotsky opens at the end of the civil war with a chapter called "The Power and the Dream," in which he described how the Bolsheviks confronted the situation they had created: "When victory was theirs at last, they found that revolutionary Russia had overreached herself and was hurled down to the bottom of a horrible pit." Seeing that the revolution had only increased their misery, the Russian people began to ask: *"Is this . . . the realm of freedom? Is this where the great leap has taken us?"* The leaders of the revolution could not answer, and retain their power. They began to equivocate and then to lie. "[While] they at first sought merely to conceal the chasm between dream and reality [they] soon insisted that the realm of freedom had already been reached—and that it lay there at the bottom of the pit. 'If people refused to believe, they had to be made to believe by force.'"[37]

So long as the revolutionaries continued to rule, they could not admit that they had made a mistake. Though they had cast an entire nation into a living hell, they had to maintain the liberating truth of the socialist Idea. And because the Idea was no longer believable, they had to make the people believe by force. It was the socialist idea that created the terror.

Because of the nature of its political mission, this terror was immeasurably greater than the repression it replaced. Whereas the czarist police had several hundred agents at its height, the Bolshevik Cheka began its career with several hundred *thousand*. Whereas the czarist secret police had operated within the framework of a rule of law, the Cheka (and its successors) did not. The czarist police repressed extralegal opponents of the political regime, that is, people who were breaking czarist law. To create the socialist future, however, the Cheka targeted whole social categories as enemies of the revolution—regardless of individual attitudes or acts—and targeted them for liquidation.

The results were predictable. "Up until 1905," wrote Aleksandr Solzhenitsyn in his searing record of the *gulag*, "the death penalty was an exceptional measure in Russia." From 1876 to 1904, 486 people were executed or seventeen people a year for the whole country (a figure which included the executions of nonpolitical criminals). During the years of the 1905 revolution and its suppression, "the number of executions rocketed upward, astounding Russian imaginations, calling forth tears from Tolstoy and . . . many others; from 1905 through 1908 about 2,200 persons were executed—forty-five a month. This, as Tagantsev said, was an *epidemic of executions*. It came to an abrupt end."[38]

But then came the Bolshevik seizure of power: "In a period of sixteen months (from June 1918 to October 1919) more than sixteen thousand persons were shot, which is to say *more than one thousand a month.*" These executions, carried out by the Cheka without trial and by revolutionary tribunals without due process, were executions of people exclusively accused of political crimes. And this was only a drop in the sea of executions to come. The true figures will never be known, but in the two years 1937 and 1938, according to the executioners themselves, half a *million* "political prisoners" were shot, or 20,000 a month.

To measure these deaths on a historical scale, Solzhenitsyn also compared them to the horrors of the Spanish Inquisition, which during the height of its existence condemned an average of 10 heretics a month.[39] The difference was this: the Inquisition only forced unbelievers to believe in a world unseen; socialism demanded that they believe in the very Lie that the revolution had condemned them to live.

The author of our century's tragedy is not Stalin, nor even Lenin. Its author is the political Left that we belonged to, that was launched at the time of Gracchus Babeuf and the Conspiracy of the Equals, and that has continued its assault on bourgeois order ever since. The reign of socialist terror is the responsibility of all those who have promoted the socialist Idea, which required so much blood to implement, and then did not work.

If socialism was a mistake, however, it was never merely innocent in the sense that its consequences could not have been foreseen. Before Marxists had spilled their first blood, the critics of Marx had warned that his schemes would end in tyranny, and would not work. In 1844, Marx's collaborator Arnold Ruge predicted that Marx's dream would result in "a police and slave state." And in 1872, the anarchist Mikhail Bakunin, Marx's archrival in the First International, described the political life of the future that Marx had in mind:

> This government will not content itself with administering and governing the masses politically, as all governments do today. It will also administer the

masses economically, concentrating in the hands of the State the production and division of wealth, the cultivation of land. . . . All that will demand . . . the reign of *scientific intelligence,* the most aristocratic, despotic, arrogant, and elitist of all regimes. There will be a new class, a new hierarchy . . . the world will be divided into a minority ruling in the name of knowledge, and an immense ignorant majority. And then, woe unto the mass of ignorant ones![40]

If a leading voice in Marx's own International could see with such clarity the oppressive implications of his revolutionary idea, there was no excuse for the generations of Marxists who promoted the idea even after it had been put into practice and the blood had begun to flow. But the idea was so seductive that even Marxists who opposed the Soviet state continued to support the socialist idea, saying this was not the socialism that Marx had in mind, even though Bakunin had seen that it was.

So powerful was the socialist fantasy that even those on the Left whom Bakunin inspired and who opposed the Communists, could not bring themselves to abandon the idea that had put the civilized West under siege. Like Bakunin, they were sworn enemies of capitalism, the only industrial system that was democratic and that worked. Their remedies for its deficiencies—abolishing private property and the economic market—would have led to generalized poverty and revolutionary terror as surely as those of Marx. By promoting the socialist idea of the future and by participating in the war against the capitalist present, these non-Marxist soldiers of the political Left became ideological partners in the very tragedies they deplored.

Of all Marx's critics, only the partisans of bourgeois order understood the mistake that socialists had made. They appreciated—as socialists did not—the only practical, and therefore real, social bases of human freedom: private property and economic markets. As the Bolsheviks completed the consolidation of their political power, the Austrian economist Ludwig von Mises, in 1922, published his classic indictment of the socialist idea and its destructive consequences. Von Mises already knew that socialism could not work and that no amount of bloodshed and repression could prevent its eventual collapse. "The problem of economic calculation," he wrote, "is the fundamental problem of socialism" and cannot be solved by socialist means. "Everything brought forward in favor of Socialism during the last hundred years, . . . all the blood which has been spilt by the supporters of socialism, cannot make socialism workable." Advocates of socialism might continue "to paint the evils of Capitalism in lurid colors" and to contrast them with an enticing picture of socialist blessings, "but all this cannot alter the fate of the socialist idea."[41] Von Mises's thesis was elaborated and extended by Friedrich Hayek, who argued that the information conveyed through the pricing system was so complex and was changing so dynamically that no planning authority, even with the aid of the most powerful computers conceivable, could ever succeed in replacing the market.[42]

Across the vast empire of societies that have put the socialist idea to the test, its fate is now obvious to all. Von Mises and Hayek, and the other prophets of capitalist economy, are now revered throughout the Soviet bloc, even as the names of Marx, Lenin and Trotsky are despised. Their works, once circulated only in *samizdat,* were among the first of *glasnost* to be unbanned. Yet, in the progressive press in the West, in articles like yours and in the efforts of your comrades to analyze the "meaning" of the Communist crisis, the arguments of the capitalist critics of socialism, who long ago demonstrated its impossibility and who have now been proven correct, are nowhere considered. As if they had never been made.

For socialists, like you, to confront these arguments would be to confront the lesson of the history that has passed: the socialist idea has been, in its consequences, one of the worst and most destructive fantasies to ever have taken hold of the minds of men.

And, despite your protestations, it *is* the idea that Marx conceived. For two hundred years, the Promethean project of the Left has been just this: to abolish property and overthrow the market, and thereby to establish the reign of reason and justice embodied in a social plan. "In Marxist utopianism, communism is the society in which things are thrown from the saddle and cease to ride mankind. Men struggle free from their own machinery and subdue it to human needs and definitions."[43] That is

Edward Thompson's summary of Marx's famous text in the first volume of *Capital:*

> The life-process of society, which is based on the process of material production, does not strip off its mystical veil until it is treated as production by freely associated men, and is consciously regulated by them in accordance with a settled plan.[44]

The "fetishism of commodities" embodied in the market is, in Marx's vision, the economic basis of the alienation at the heart of man's estate, "a definite social relation between men, that assumes, in their eyes, the fantastic form of a relation between things."[45] The aim of socialist liberation is mankind's reappropriation of its own activity and its own product—the reappropriation of man by man—that can only be achieved when private property and the market are replaced by a social plan.

The slogan Marx inscribed on the banners of the Communist future, "from each according to his ability to each according to his need," is really an expropriated version of Adam Smith's Invisible Hand, under which the pursuit of individual interest leads to the fulfillment of the interests of all. But, in the socialist future, there is no market to rule over individual human passions and channel self-interest into social satisfaction, just as there is no rule of law to protect individual rights from the human passions that rule the state. There is only the unmediated power of the socialist vanguard, which it now exercises from its bureaucratic throne.

All the theorizing about socialist liberation comes down to this: The inhabitants of the new society will be freed from the constraints of markets and the guidelines of tradition and bourgeois notions of a rule of law. They will be masters in their own house and makers of their own fate. But this liberation is, finally, a Faustian bargain. Because it will not work. Moreover, the effort to make it work will create a landscape of human suffering as great as any ever imagined.

————

Toward the end of his life, our friend Isaac Deutscher had a premonition of the disaster that has now overtaken the socialist Left. In the conclusion to the final volume of his Trotsky trilogy, *The Prophet Outcast,* he speculated on the fate that would befall his revolutionary hero if the socialist project itself should fail:

> If the view were to be taken that all that the Bolsheviks aimed at—socialism—was no more than a *fata morgana,* that the revolution merely substituted one kind of exploitation and oppression for another, and could not do otherwise, then Trotsky would appear as the high priest of a god that was bound to fail, as Utopia's servant mortally entangled in his dreams and illusions.

But Deutscher did not have the strength to see the true dimensions of the catastrophe that socialism had in store. Instead, his realism only served to reveal the depths of self-delusion and self-justifying romanticism that provide sustenance for the Left. Even if such a failure were to take place, he argued, the revolutionary hero, "would [still] attract the respect and sympathy due to the great utopians and visionaries. . . .

> Even if it were true that it is man's fate to stagger in pain and blood from defeat to defeat and to throw off one yoke only to bend his neck beneath another—even then man's longings for a different destiny would still, like pillars of fire, relieve the darkness and gloom of the endless desert through which he has been wandering with no promised land beyond.[46]

This is the true self-vision of the Left: an army of saints on the march against injustice, lacking, itself, the capacity for evil. The Left sees its revolutions as pillars of fire that light up humanity's deserts, but burn no civilizations as they pass. It lacks the ability to make the most basic moral accounting, the awareness that the Marxes, Trotskys, and Lenins immeasurably increased the suffering of humanity, and destroyed many of the blooms that existing civilizations had managed to put forth.

The quest for a new world consumed the lives of entire nations. The effort to produce a super race of socialist men and women created monstrosities instead. And these horrors were predictable, indeed *were* predicted by critics who saw that the radical ideals would create the very demons that ultimately consumed them.

For behind the revolutionary pursuit of the impossible ideal lies a deep hatred for the human norm, an unquenchable desire for its annihilation. It was the *in*humanity of our radical ambition that made the evil of the Communist epoch so total. Self-hatred is the dark side of the ambition to exceed all previous human possibility, and the ultimate root of the revolutionary ideal. Totalitarian terror is the necessary means for an agenda whose aim is to erase the past and remake the human soul. The totalitarian state was not an aberration of the progressive spirit, but its consummation. The radical project is a war against nature.

This is the reason that the socialist effort to reconstruct humanity achieved Orwellian results, the promise of freedom a terrorist state; the promise of wealth a minimalist existence. In the end, the Adams and Eves of the liberated future proved to be only grotesque masks of their pre-Revolutionary selves. It was their all-too-human desires that shaped the socialist terror, while the old humanity reasserted itself the instant the terror was removed.

Why should we have expected anything different? What else could have resulted from so calculated a rupture with the human past? What positive outcome could be achieved by so radical a rejection of tradition, and the wholesale destruction of existing institutions? What could an experiment like this produce *other* than a social Frankenstein?

Yet, without socialism, the peoples of the Russian Empire might have moved into the front ranks of the modern industrial world (like the Japanese) without the incalculable human cost. Instead, even the most productive of the Soviet satellites, East Germany, once the Prussian powerhouse of European industrialism, is now condemned to a blighted economic standard below that of Italy, South Korea or Spain.

Consider now the history of our century. On whose heads does the responsibility lie for the blood that was shed to make the socialist experiment possible? If the socialist idea is a chimera and the revolutionary path a road to nowhere, can the revolutions themselves be noble, even in intention? Can they be justified by the lesser but known evils they sought to redress?

Consider: if no one had believed Marx's idea, there would have been no Bolshevik Revolution; Russia might have evolved into a modern, democratic, industrial state; Hitler would not have come to power; there would have been no Cold War. For seventy years, the revolutionary Left put its weight on the totalitarian side in the international civil war that Lenin had launched, and against the side that promoted human freedom and industrial progress. And it did so in the name of an idea that could not work.

The communist idea is not the principle of the modern world, as Marx supposed, but its antiprinciple, the reactionary rejection of political individualism and the market economies of the liberal West. Wherever the revolutionary Left has triumphed, its triumph has meant economic backwardness and social poverty, cultural deprivation and the loss of political freedom for all those unfortunate peoples under its yoke.

This is the real legacy of the Left of which you and I were a part. We called ourselves progressives; but we were the true reactionaries of the modern world.

The Iron Curtain that divided the prisoners of socialism from the free men and women of the West has now been torn down. The iron curtain that divides us remains. It is the utopian dream that is so destructive and that you refuse to give up.

Your ex-comrade,
David

CHAPTER THREE

THE RELIGIOUS
ROOTS OF
RADICALISM

Mr. Marx does not believe in God, but he believes
deeply in himself. His heart is filled not with love
but with rancor. He has very little benevolence
toward men and becomes . . . furious and . . .
spiteful . . . when anyone dares question the omni-
science of the divinity whom he adores, that is to
say, Mr. Marx himself.

—Mikhail Bakunin, 1872

AS AN ORTHODOX JEW IN PREWAR POLAND,[1] THE MARXIST
historian Isaac Deutscher found himself captivated by a passage in the
Midrash about Rabbi Meir, the great disciple of Rabbi Akiva. The passage
described how Rabbi Meir took lessons in theology from a heretic called
Akher (The Other). On one particular Sabbath, as Deutscher recalled,

"Rabbi Meir was with his teacher, and as usual they became engaged in a deep argument. The heretic was riding a donkey, and Rabbi Meir, as he could not ride on a Sabbath, walked by his side and listened so intently to the words of wisdom falling from his heretical lips that he failed to notice that he and his teacher had reached the ritual boundary which Jews were not allowed to cross on a Sabbath. The great heretic turned to his Orthodox pupil and said: 'Look, we have reached the boundary—we must part now; you must not accompany me any farther—go back!' Rabbi Meir went back to the Jewish community, while the heretic rode on—beyond the boundaries of Jewry."[2]

Deutscher was fascinated with the story. "Why," he wondered, "did Rabbi Meir, that leading light of Orthodoxy, take his lessons from the heretic? . . . Why did he defend him against other rabbis? . . . Who was he? He appeared to be in Jewry and yet out of it. He showed a curious respect for his pupil's Orthodoxy when he sent him back to the Jews on the Holy Sabbath; but he himself, disregarding canon and ritual, rode beyond the boundaries."

In the figure of the heretical stranger, Deutscher saw a paradigm for his own radical career. The Jewish heretic who crosses boundaries and transcends their limits, Deutscher wrote, is the prototype of the modern revolutionary. By way of defining the revolutionary tradition to which he himself belonged, he identified its exponents: Spinoza, Marx, Rosa Luxemburg, Trotsky. These famous revolutionary heretics "found Jewry too narrow, too archaic, and too constricting," and therefore "looked for ideals and fulfillment beyond it." In the secular world they entered, they were outsiders as well: "They lived on the margins or in the nooks and crannies of their respective nations. Each of them was in society and yet not in it, of it and yet not of it." Living beyond invisible boundaries made them almost godlike: "It . . . enabled them to rise in thought above their societies, above their nations, above their times and generations, and to strike out mentally into wide new horizons and far into the future."

Isaac Deutscher was my teacher, and Akher, the heretical stranger, is a figure with whom I came to identify in my life as a radical. I was the scion of socialists and Communists, of Jews estranged from Judaism who pursued ideals beyond the limits of the Jewish community and its traditions, of revolutionaries who pursued fulfillment in a liberated future beyond the confines of the societies and nations that defined the human present. When I was nine, I remember marching with my parents in a Communist May Day Parade in New York City. The year was 1948, and Communist political forces directed by Moscow and backed by the Red Army were taking control of Eastern Europe. In February, the Communists had overthrown the government of Czechoslovakia. In March, President Truman went before Congress to mobilize America's forces for the anti-Communist battles that loomed ahead. It was the beginning of the Cold War, and our May Day parade was an act of political defiance.

My parents and I were already on the other side of invisible boundaries—boundaries that separated us from the nation on whose margin, and in whose nooks and crannies we lived. And yet, as we chanted our slogans—"One, two, three, four / We don't want another war"—we felt anything but homeless. In marching in these ranks, we had crossed another boundary into a realm of our political imaginations, where the revolutionary future was already here. In our hearts, we felt an immense, reassuring pride to be part of the vanguard of progressive humanity, marching toward a world in which war and injustice would be only memories of the past.

Along the route down New York's Eighth Avenue, gray wooden barriers with black stenciled letters N.Y.P.D. lined the sidewalks to hold back the crowds of hostile onlookers. My fear was held at bay by a pressure in the lungs from our chants and songs. At one point, our ranks fell silent as we stopped to let the cross traffic pass. As we waited to resume our march, a group of street kids, some no bigger than I, leaned over one of the barriers and began to chant: "Down with the Communists! Up with the Irish!" The taunt wounded and confused me, as though an actual blow had been delivered. A hurt stuck in my throat: it was so *unjust.* I wanted to cry back: *You don't understand! We're doing this for you. For Irish and non-Irish alike. For the day when there won't be any wars and there won't be any nations. Just one human family.* I wanted to respond, but I didn't. All day, I had been chanting into the air with the others to an invisible audience, whom I was sure needed to hear the truth we were telling and would welcome it. Now I was confronted by real people who heard what we had to say and who despised and hated us for it.

This is the only clear memory I have of that entire May Day in 1948. For the next twenty-five years, I remained in the ranks of the political Left. I was a soldier in an international army fighting on behalf of the poor and the oppressed. I had taken on the cause of all the communities of the dispossessed. It was only much later that I came to realize that in becoming part of the Left I had really taken on the cause of no community at all. Though we were in society, we were not of it. We represented no one, not even ourselves. In all those years of championing the oppressed, it would never once have occurred to me, for example, to shout out, like those Irish kids: *Up with the Jews!*

I did not identify myself as a Jew. I was a revolutionary and an internationalist. To see myself as a Jew—a member of a real community in all its human limits, with all its human faults—to identify with the claims of such a community, would have been a betrayal of the revolutionary Idea. In all those years, I never allowed myself to explore what it might mean to have a real sense of myself as a Jew, just as I never really felt myself to be an American, or to identify with any community less extensive than humanity itself. In this attitude, I was typical of the Left. It was only after I finally gave up the revolutionary fantasy that I began for the first time to experience my own reality and the reality of the communities to which I belonged—only when I had left the ranks of the political vanguard whose mission it was to change the world.

When I did leave the Left, the moral I drew from the *Midrash* story of Rabbi Meir and the heretical stranger that so impressed Isaac Deutscher, was no longer *his* moral. It was quite opposite. The moral I take from it now is the importance of boundaries—the religious boundaries that separate the holy from the profane; the secular boundaries that separate the uncharted from the familiar, the apocalyptic from the mundane. Among the conservative lessons my heretical life has taught me about boundaries are the costs incurred in crossing them.

When I was starting out as a radical in the 1960s, Deutscher was already a celebrated cultural figure as the Marxist biographer of Trotsky and Stalin. Forty years earlier, when the Bolshevik Revolution was still young, Deutscher had been a political activist in Eastern Europe. Later, as a mentor to New Leftists like me, Deutscher was always ready with an instructive anecdote about those intoxicating times. One of his amusing parables concerned the two most important leaders of the Communist International, Karl Radek and Grigory Zinoviev, who had come to Germany in 1918 to stoke the fires of revolution. Like many other leading Bolsheviks (Sverdlov, Kamenev and Trotsky, for example), both Radek and Zinoviev were Jews, as was the foremost figure of the German Revolution—Rosa Luxemburg—and the head of the new revolutionary government in Hungary, Béla Kun. And, of course, the inspirer of all their revolutionary exertions, Karl Marx himself, had come from a long line of famous rabbis in Trier.

Radek was addressing the crowd. "We have had the Revolution in Russia and the Revolution in Hungary, and now the Revolution is erupting in Germany," he roared, "and after that we will have the Revolution in France and the Revolution in England and the Revolution in America." As Radek worked up his passion, Zinoviev tapped him on the shoulder and whispered, "Karl, Karl, there won't be enough Jews to go around."

The story is apocryphal, but the point is telling. For nearly two hundred years, Jews have played a disproportionate role as leaders of the modern revolutionary movements in Europe and the West. In the eyes of these socialist revolutionaries, the bourgeois freedom established by the French Revolution was only half freedom. The universal Rights of Man created a unity of mankind in the political realm, but had left the citizenry divided and unequal in civil society. Only a new revolution could make whole the defect in the social cosmos. By carrying the revolution to its conclusion, socialists would usher in a millennium and fulfill the messianic prophecies of the pre-Enlightenment religions that modern ideas had discredited. Through this revolution, the lost unity of mankind would be restored, social harmony would be reestablished, paradise regained. It would be a *tikkun olam,* a repair of the world.

If the revolution was a secular faith, its Moses was a deracinated Jew whose father had changed his name from Herschel to Heinrich, and converted to Christianity to advance his government career. The young

Marx grew into a brilliant but rancorous adult, consumed by hatred not only for the society that disdained him, but for the community that had raised him. Internalizing the worst anti-Semitic stereotypes, he incorporated them into his early revolutionary vision, identifying Jews as symbols of the society he wanted to destroy: "The god of the Jews has been secularized and has become the god of this world," he wrote in one of his early manuscripts. "Money is the jealous God of Israel, beside which no other God may stand." In a catechism for revolutionaries, he took on the voice of his people's timeless persecutors: "What is the secular basis of Judaism? Practical need, selfishness. What is the secular cult of the Jew? Haggling. What is his secular god? Money. . . . Money is the alienated essence of man's work and existence: this essence dominates him and he worships it." Salvation for the Jews lay in the revolution that would uproot the foundations of the social order itself. For once the revolution succeeded in "destroying the empirical essence of Judaism," Marx promised, "the Jew will become impossible, because his consciousness will no longer have an object." The revolutionary equation was thus complete: "the social emancipation of Jewry is the emancipation of society from Judaism."[3]

For secular Jews, like Marx, the radical idea that the bourgeois revolution had somehow been incomplete carried irresistible appeal. The bourgeois bill of rights had emancipated Europe's ghettos, granting civil freedom to individual Jews, but refused to recognize the Jewish people itself, which stubbornly rejected assimilation. As a result, even secularized Jews like Marx were looked on as members of an alien nation. To them, the socialist revolution promised a true restoration of their own humanity and general liberation—a society freed from religious illusion and national division; a world made whole; a *tikkun olam*. Communism, as Marx put it, was "the riddle of humanity solved"—as though the problem of human alienation and suffering was nothing more than an intellectual puzzle.

Anti-Semitism was an animating passion of the founders of socialism (Fourier and Proudhon, as well as Marx), but throughout the Nineteenth Century its poisons emanated principally from the Right, while Jews found their defenders on the political Left. But the First World War changed this. Its barbarities shattered the expectations of civil progress and revived the passions of revolt, and out of the ashes of the cataclysm new radical movements emerged.

Fascism and Communism were both rooted in the messianic ambitions and gnostic illusions that the Enlightenment had unleashed;[4] both invoked the salvationist claims of the socialist promise; both looked to a historical transcendence, proposing final solutions to what had been timeless problems of the human condition. Both set out to create their socialist futures by first destroying the bourgeois present, then erecting their utopias on its smoldering ruins. Both intended to restore the lost unity of mankind by first dividing humanity into opposing camps: the politically saved and the morally damned, the children of light and the carriers of darkness, Us and Them. Fascism proposed to build its utopia on the *Volk,* the purity and solidarity of the tribe. International socialism proposed to build its utopia on class foundations—the creation of a morally purified, proletarian *Ubermensch,* the "new man" and "new woman." The means of purification, for both messianisms, was political terror. "Proletarian coercion in all its forms, beginning with the firing squad," explained the Bolshevik Bukharin, later a victim of his own prescription, "is . . . the way of fashioning the communist man out of the human material of the capitalist era."[5]

After 1917, these movements declared political war on the liberal orders of bourgeois Europe. In Germany, the Communist Party ordered its activists to collaborate with the Nazis in political violence designed to cause the collapse of the democratic governing coalition.[6] In 1933, they succeeded in destroying the Weimar Republic, an act which settled the fate of European Jewry.

Deutscher was a soldier on one side of that political battle. In a moment of intimacy we shared as teacher and disciple, he confessed to me his guilt at having been wrong on an issue that spelled life and death for millions of Jews. Along with other Jews active in the Marxist Internationals during the interwar years, Deutscher had argued relentlessly in behalf of the self-determination of all nationalities—except Jews. In becoming revolutionary internationalists, these Jewish heretics curiously adopted a tenet of the biblical faith they had rejected. As a people without a land, they argued, Jews were endowed with a special mission in humanity's march toward the revolutionary future. The mission was to be a revolutionary "light unto the nations," to point to the redemption of man in a united world where nations themselves would no longer exist.

As Lenin's right hand in power, the Jew Trotsky (né Bronstein) had turned a deaf ear to the pleas of his own people, dismissing Soviet Jews as creatures of the despised petite bourgeoisie. In the second year of Hitler's war, Trotsky pontificated from his Mexican exile on the fate of his fellow Jews:

> The attempt to solve the Jewish question through the migration of the Jews to Palestine can now be seen for what it is, a tragic mockery of the Jewish people. . . . Never was it so clear as it is today, that the salvation of the Jewish people is bound up inseparably with the overthrow of the capitalist system.[7]

Thus, Trostky and Deutscher and the other internationalists argued within the Jewish community in the Thirties that its salvation lay in the overthrow of capitalism, that the solution to the "Jewish problem" was the Marxist revolution, in other words, the destruction of liberal society in Europe. They argued against those Zionists in the socialist movement who urged Jews to emigrate to Palestine and the nascent Jewish state as a place of refuge and an ark of survival; and they argued against all those nonsocialists who struggled to shore up the liberal democracies of the capitalist West as bulwarks against the barbarian threat.

By working to destroy these liberal societies and to undermine their bourgeois rights, radicals like Deutscher and Trotsky helped to remove the life supports of European Jewry. But the revolutionary salvation they promised never came. Only the handful who disregarded their appeals and went to Palestine to build a Zionist state survived; the multitudes who heeded them and their comrades, and stayed to fight for socialism, perished in the Nazi Holocaust.

In Russia itself, hardly a single one of the Bolshevik Jews survived the Stalinist terror: Radek, Zinoviev, Kamenev, Sverdlov and Trotsky all were murdered by the revolution in which they had placed their faith. Still, the bulk of Soviet Jewry survived the Nazi invasion, a fact that fed the illusion that socialism might still offer the Jews hope. But as soon as the war was over, Stalin began preparing his own "final solution" to complete the job that Hitler had started. In 1948, the arrests and murders of Soviet Jews began, and only Stalin's death prevented the new holocaust from running its course.[8]

Stalin's campaign against the Jews was inspired by his own paranoia, but its rationale remained well within the parameters of the socialist project. Lenin himself had written: "Whoever, directly or indirectly, puts forward the slogan of a Jewish 'national culture' (whatever his good intentions may be), is an enemy of the proletariat, a supporter of the *old* . . . an accomplice of the rabbis and the bourgeoisie. . . ."[9] Or, in Marx's own formula: "In the last analysis, the emancipation of the Jews is the emancipation of mankind from Judaism." Stalin's anti-Semitic heirs continued their cultural and religious assault on the Jewish community, as on all minorities within their socialist empire, training the terrorists and supplying the arsenals with which the Arab enemies of Israel threatened the survival of the Jewish state.

Once, the locus of international anti-Semitism was on the Right; today it is on the Left. The two havens of post-Holocaust Jewry, Israel and the United States, are the two states that have been under assault by the international Left almost since the end of World War II. "U.S. imperialism" and "Zionist racism" are the Great Satans of leftist imagination. Within the United States, the PLO and other Arab terrorists have struck alliances with racist and anti-Semitic black "nationalists" like Louis Farrakhan, while allies of Farrakhan have become part of the "progressive" rainbow of the Democratic Party. And prominent, still, in this broad movement of the contemporary Left are Jews laboring under the same illusion as the Jewish radicals of the past: that they are a light unto the nations; that their revolution will bring about a messianic transformation of communal hatred into socialist harmony, human evil into social good; that it will mean a *tikkun olam*.[10]

What accounts for the persistence of this self-destructive commitment to the messianic ambitions of the revolutionary Left? Why, in the face of its practical catastrophes, does the Left continue to attract so many idealists, and Jewish idealists in particular?

An answer frequently given is the ethical affinity between socialism and Judaism. In this view, socialism is the fulfillment of the moral teachings of the Jewish prophets; socialists are the compassionate angels of the secular world. But what is moral or angelic about a movement that aligns itself with anti-Semites and racists, and advances its agendas behind a veil of deception? What is compassionate about a cause that gave the world the *gulag* and the politically instigated famine, that spawned the generalized misery of the socialist world? To say that the revolutionary promise of social justice is what attracts Jews to the Left is only to identify a self-delusion. It does not explain why Jews continue to feel at home there, despite the grim record of leftist practice. To explain this, one must first understand the nature of this secular faith. For to sustain belief in the face of such contradiction requires, above all, an act of faith.

As others have recognized, revolutionary hope is a religious gnosticism.[11] It is the belief in a world possessed by evil and an earthly redemption achieved through knowledge. The Left is impervious to its own catastrophes because the perception of catastrophe is the very premise of its faith. The religious foundation of its political beliefs is the idea of history as a fall from grace. If a socialist experiment proves to be corrupt, this is merely its failure to escape existing corruption. The Left is not satisfied to reform particular institutions. It proposes, instead, to rectify the general catastrophe of existence itself. Until the general redemption is achieved, particular solutions will be meaningless, and easy to undo.

To the secular messianists of the radical Left, the world we know is a social illusion. Mankind is alienated from its "true self." Likewise, to the religious gnostic, reality is a delusion, a creation of false consciousness. The religious revolutionary believes that humanity creates its own reality. There is no limit, therefore, to what humanity may become. Alienation and suffering can actually be abolished by a revolution that restores humanity to its authentic being. Reactionary religion, by contrast, tries to reconcile humanity to its unacceptable reality with a dream of divine intervention and otherworldly hope. It is the opium of the people, projecting humanity's own power—which is the power to redeem itself—onto a supernatural being, God. The revolutionary faith rejects the illusion of divine grace and proposes *itself* as the messianic force. The revolutionary answer to the religious question is the demand to change the conditions that make religion necessary. The revolutionary prophet proclaims a liberation theology: *You shall be as gods, creating the conditions of your own redemption.*

"Alienation" is the Marxist name for the catastrophe that has befallen human existence, for the fact that there are not merely particular injustices to be remedied by specific reforms, but that there is injustice in the very structure of mankind's being in the world, that no mere reform can heal. Jews have a name for this catastrophe of existence too, and it is the same name: *Exile.* In Marx's *Communist Manifesto* the proletariat is identified as a people in exile like the Jews: "Proletarians have no country. . . . Proletarians of the world unite; you have nothing to lose but your chains."

The political prelude to the First World War refuted Marx's proclamation. When war was declared, the socialist parties aligned themselves with their respective nations, proving that proletarians did have a *patria* and thus more to lose than their chains. Exile was not the real condition of proletarians, but it *was* the real condition of Jews like Marx. Self-excluded from his own community as a religious expatriate, excluded from German society as a Jew, self-excluded again as a socialist revolutionary in bourgeois England, Marx conceived his internationalist dream to solve this riddle. Socialism was the wish to free himself from his personal exile by destroying the very idea of nations, by uniting mankind in a Marxist Zion.[12]

It is the paradigm of exile that links the fate of the Jews to the radical Left. The same paradigm forges the false bonds between Jewish faith and revolutionary fervor. And it is the paradigm of exile in the Jewish tradition that warns us of the dangers of such messianic hopes—hopes that are gnostic and apocalyptic, that propose a self-transformation of men into angels, and that promise the establishment of paradise on earth.

IN THE JEWISH tradition, an exile stands at the threshold of all human history: the expulsion of the first couple from the Garden of Eden. Adam and Eve were our parents, but they did not know good and evil,

shame and suffering, labor and death. They are our parents and our innocence; we are of them, but we are not like them. They are what we dream
of being.

Genesis is a cautionary tale of who we are. In its Garden, only one
fruit was forbidden: "Of the tree of the knowledge of good and evil you
shall not eat, for in the day that you eat of it you shall die." To eat from
this tree was to lose innocence and thus the very paradise that had been
given. But after God had warned them, the serpent came to Eve and, in
words that are almost exactly the words of the Marxist promise, urged her
to disregard what God had commanded: "For . . . when you eat of it your
eyes will be opened, and you will be like God, . . ." So Adam and Eve ate
the forbidden fruit and God punished them, causing them to bear children in pain and to toil all the days of their lives, until death.

There was a further penalty, expulsion from paradise:

> Then the Lord God said, "Behold, the man has become like one of us,
> knowing good and evil; and now, lest he put forth his hand and take also of
> the tree of life, and eat, and live forever"—therefore the Lord God sent him
> forth from the garden of Eden, to till the ground from which he was taken.
> He drove out the man; and at the source, the garden of Eden, he placed an
> angel, and a sword of the spirit which turned every way, to guard the way to
> the tree of life.

In this parable, the possibility of redemption is symbolized by the flam-
ing sword that points the way back. But, by barring entrance, the sword
also symbolizes that return is possible only through a divine grace.

In the biblical tradition, the expulsion from paradise is the threshold
of human history. God's curse—to live in exile from paradise, to labor in
pain, to suffer and die—can be translated thus: *You shall be human.* The
moment that our common parents eat from the tree of knowledge, mix-
ing good and evil, we are human: permanently exiled from our origins,
perpetually estranged from ourselves.

The theme of exile recurs through biblical history. Not long after the
first couple were banished from Eden, the Bible relates that God was
again so provoked by the spectacle of human mischief that He decided to

expel His creation from the earth itself. ("The Lord saw that the wickedness of man was great in the earth. . . . So the Lord said, 'I will blot out man whom I have created from the face of the ground. . . .'") But one man, Noah, found favor with God for his goodness, and God relented, deciding to spare Noah, saying "I will establish my covenant with you. . . ."

After the flood that God sent to destroy the world, Noah built an altar and made an offering. When Noah had done this, God was ready, as a wise if rueful parent, to reconcile himself to His own creation: "When the Lord smelled the pleasing odor [of Noah's offering], the Lord said in his heart, 'I will never again curse the ground because of man, for the imagination of man's heart is evil from his youth; neither will I ever again destroy every living creature as I have done.'"

Here, in the first of those remarkable self-bindings of the divine power in Jewish tradition, God sets the boundaries of human existence, declaring that He will live with His creation, destined though His creatures are to disappoint Him and to do evil. This is the first covenant, which, in the course of the exodus from Egypt, becomes a covenant between God and His people, Israel. Later, in the Sinai wilderness, God tells the Israelites, "You shall be unto me a kingdom of priests and a holy nation." But even though they are chosen, the Israelites remain children of Adam, in whose hearts good and evil are confused.

Because they are chosen, God provides the Israelites with a path back toward the source. This path is the Law that God first gives to Moses at Sinai. In Eden, before the Fall, there was but one commandment. Now there are many. Lest their essential meaning be forgotten, God tells His prophet: "Speak to the children of Israel and tell them to make for themselves fringes on the corners of their garments throughout their generations, and to put on the fringe of each corner a blue thread." The fringe signifies the boundary they must observe to keep their human hearts in check: "You shall have it as a fringe so that when you look upon it you will remember to do all the commands of the Lord, and you will not follow the desires of your heart and your eyes which lead you astray." Human beings are still the children of Adam and Eve, creatures prone to evil through the desires of the heart.

God's covenant is two-edged, like the sword that guards the gates of Eden, both blessing and curse:

> See, I have set before you this day life and good, death and evil. If you obey the commandments of the Lord your God which I command you this day, by loving the Lord your God, by walking in His ways, and by keeping His commandments and His statutes and His ordinances, then you shall live and multiply, and the Lord your God will bless you in the land which you are entering to take possession of it. But if your heart turns away, and you will not hear, . . . you shall perish; . . . [I will] scatter you among the nations . . . the land of your enemies shall eat you up.[13]

Exile is God's curse for breaking His covenant, for choosing evil over good. But because God is bound by His own covenant not to destroy his creation, this exile is also the ground of hope. To those whose hearts are open to God and who keep His commandments, there is the promise of a return to the source.

Throughout the early exiles of the Israelites, this hope of redemption is bound up with the coming of a *messiah,* one anointed by God, like David, to lead the return of God's people to their home in Zion. But as the exile from the Land of Israel becomes more and more permanent, an apocalyptic strain develops in Jewish messianism, which no longer conceives the event as a restoration of the good of a previous time. Before, the vision of the messianic future was summarized by a saying in the Talmud: "The only difference between this eon and the Days of the Messiah is the subjection [of Israel] to the nations." But now the prophets begin to speak, instead, of an "End of Days," whose coming will be miraculous and sudden, in which God Himself will reign and establish His law, and which will signal an end to historical time.

Even this apocalyptic messianism, however, did not forget the meaning of history: in God and His covenant lie the sole hope of man's redemption. Thus, the cornerstone of the prayer service of diaspora Jewry, the *Amidah,* is a paean to the God of Abraham, Isaac and Jacob, which celebrates the covenant and its promise: "Blessed art Thou, O Lord, the Redeemer of Israel. . . . Blow the Great Shofar for our freedom, and lift up a banner to gather our exiles, and gather us from the four corners of the earth. Blessed art Thou, O Lord, who gatherest the banished of Thy people Israel."

The humility of defeat, the suffering of exile, teaches us who we are. It is no coincidence that the great formative periods of the Jewish religion—the time of the Patriarchs, of the revelation at Sinai, of the compilation of the Talmud—are all periods of Jewish exile. But there is a danger in exile too. Its sufferings can become so terrible that we forget the truth behind the covenant: We are children of Adam, destined by what we are to confuse good and evil; condemned by who we are to dwell far from the source in Eden. Forgetting who we are, we no longer struggle within the terms of the condition we have inherited to make ourselves better and more just; instead, we rebel against the condition of exile itself. In search of an entirely new kind of redemption, we turn to mystical knowledge and miraculous faiths, to false gods and self-anointed messiahs.

After the destruction of the Second Temple, as hundreds of years of Israel's persecution and exile grew to be thousands, Jews in the diaspora began to ask themselves unthinkable questions: How could God have chosen the Jews and then abandoned them? How could God's chosen people deserve such punishment? How can God *be* God and yet such evil exist? These questions were really one question: How can our exile be explained?

About the time of the Renaissance in Europe, a group of Jewish mystics living in Palestine formulated an answer. In so doing, they developed a view radically different from traditional views of the Jewish exile and of the messianic redemption as well. In the Kabbalistic teaching of Isaac Luria and his disciples, God Himself became part of the exile of His people, and God's self-exile the explanation for how evil entered the world.[14]

Before Eden, according to the Lurianic teaching, there was a primal act of creation. God withdrew into himself, creating the nothingness, the non-God, out of which the world was created. Thus, in Lurianic gnosticism, there was no longer one divine creation, in which God's children chose freely between what is right and what is wrong, but a creation dominated by warring forces of good and evil. The elements of this creation are the *Sefirot,* or vessels of emanated light radiating the plenitude of the divine influence. According to Luria, during the primal act of creation only the first three levels of *Sefirot* could adequately contain the primal "divine light." When the radiation reached the six lower *Sefirot,* their capacity failed and they were shattered by the radiance. Sparks of the divine light were trapped in the fragments of these vessels, and some mounted aloft, while others descended and sank. Those that sank, the *Kelippot,* or husks, were transformed into the forces of impurity and evil, whose strength derives from the sparks of divine light that are still trapped within them.

This is the Lurianic exile—the light entrapped within the broken vessels and subjected to evil. No longer is it an exile merely of the children of Adam, but of God Himself; no longer are the Israelites alone in their exile: the *Shekhina,* the divine presence, dwells in exile with them. For in the course of its creation, the universe itself has become flawed. Its flaw is a flaw in man *and* God, in creation itself. To heal the wound in creation requires a *tikkun olam*—a repair of the world.

This *tikkun olam* is the new Lurianic doctrine of redemption. The *Shekhina* must be reunited with God. The task of reunion is given to the people whom God has chosen. Redemption takes place through the holiness of the Chosen, whose observances and prayers are performed with a mystical intensity that deprives evil of its power. By redeeming the divine light, they perfect not only the soul of the Jewish people but of the whole world. For when the sparks that are trapped in the broken vessels are liberated and returned to their source, the Exile of the Light comes to an end, and the human and cosmic redemption is achieved.

What has happened in this Kabbalistic revision of the meaning of exile is the transformation of the religious teaching into a gnostic creed: redemption is no longer a divine release from the punishment of exile, but a humanly inspired transformation of creation itself.[15] The concept of human exile has become divorced from the realities of history, the attempt to restore a covenant broken through humanity's continuing capacity for evil. It has become instead a mystical Idea: the liberation of the divine light that will make the cosmos whole. In the gnostic view, the evil that men do emanates not from their own flawed natures, but is the result of a flaw in the cosmos they inhabit, which they can repair. Man is his own redeemer.

Thus, the meaning of human exile is dramatically—and demonically—transformed. It is no longer a punishment, but a mission; no longer a reflection of who we are, but a mark of our destiny to become agents of salvation. In this gnostic vision, Israel is dispersed among the nations *in order* that the light of the whole world may be liberated. In the words of the Kabbalist Hayim Vital: "This is the secret why Israel is fated to be enslaved by all the Gentiles of the world: In order that it may uplift those sparks [of the Divine Light] which have also fallen among them. . . . And therefore it was necessary that Israel should be scattered to the four winds in order to lift everything up."[16] The Israelites are the first revolutionary internationalists.

Gnostic messianism is the echo of that serpentine voice that seduced Eve and led Adam to his Fall: *You shall be redeemers; you shall be as God.*

In the years following the expulsion of the Jews from Spain during the time of Columbus, the new doctrines of Isaac Luria spread rapidly. Then, in 1648, the year of the Chmielnicki massacres, a tormented mystic named Shabbtai Zvi appeared in Smyrna, claiming to be the true Messiah. For seventeen years, no one paid attention to his pathetic claims. An eccentric, manic-depressive, Zvi was given to blasphemies in his ecstatic states, pronouncing the forbidden name of God, violating Jewish law and holding a mystic marriage with the Torah under a wedding canopy. He often invoked the benediction "To Him who allows the forbidden."

For his heresies, Shabbtai Zvi was expelled in turn from Smyrna, Salonika and Constantinople and would have been forgotten, except that, finally recognizing that he was sick, he decided to seek the help of a brilliant young Kabbalist in Jerusalem, hoping the scholar would be able to exorcise the demons that afflicted him. This Kabbalist was Nathan of Gaza.

Nathan of Gaza was the prototype of the Jewish revolutionary gnostic whose tradition culminated in Marx. Instead of attempting to cure Shabbtai Zvi, he reinterpreted his dementia and disobedience as signs that the messianic hour was indeed at hand, the point at which human history passes beyond good and evil. In 1665, Nathan of Gaza proclaimed the madman Shabbtai Zvi to be the true Messiah, and devised a new doctrine of creation to justify his choice.

According to this doctrine, when some sparks of the divine light fell into the abyss following the breaking of the vessels, the soul of the Messiah, embedded in the original divine light, also fell. The soul of the Messiah dwelt in the depth of the great abyss, held in the prison of the *Kelippot,* the realm of darkness. Drawing on the fact that the Hebrew word for "serpent" *(Nahash)* has the same numerical value in Kabbalistic doctrine as the word for "messiah" *(Mosiach),* Nathan identified the Messiah as the "holy serpent" of this darkness. Only when the historical process of perfection was complete would the soul of the Messiah leave its dark prison and reveal itself to the world. Only to the degree that the process of the *tikkun* of all the world liberated the good from evil in the depth of the primal space would the soul of the Messiah be freed from its bondage.[17] Shabbtai Zvi's violation of the laws, far from disqualifying him as one anointed by God, were the sure signs that he was engaged in a messianic mission.

There had been other Messiah claimants before Shabbtai Zvi. But they had no prophet, like Nathan of Gaza, to anoint them, and no dialectical science, like the Lurianic doctrine, to sanctify them. Shabbtai Zvi, who had been previously dismissed as a man deranged, now was endorsed by the rabbinate, becoming the repository of messianic hope for Jewish communities from Frankfurt to Jerusalem. No one now believed in Shabbtai Zvi more than he himself. He announced the very date of redemption for June 18, 1666, and, proclaiming the imminent deposition of the Turkish sultan, sailed for Constantinople. But when his ship reached Turkish waters in February 1666, the Messiah was arrested and put in chains. Brought before the sultan and given the choice of death or conversion to Islam, the Jewish Messiah renounced his faith.

After the apostasy, the betrayed communities of diaspora Jewry were overcome with confusion and despair, and the institutions of Orthodoxy drew a veil of silence over what had transpired. But a hard core of believers remained unshaken and undaunted, and the rump of the Shabbatian movement survived. Nathan of Gaza explained the apostasy of the Messiah in dialectical fashion as the beginning of a new mission to release the divine sparks scattered among the gentiles, to redeem the light entrapped in Islamic darkness: it was the Messiah's task to take on the appearance of evil in order to purify others.

IN THE GNOSTIC messianism of Nathan of Gaza and Shabbtai Zvi, in the antinomian belief in redemption through sin, in the arrogant ambition to transform human nature and remake the world, and in the very self-anointing presumption of a messianic party lies the true ancestry of the revolutionary Left.

The gnostic vision of exile—the light entrapped and subjected to evil—is precisely the Enlightenment vision of human oppression and liberation, which Marx and the socialists inherited. Man is born free, but is everywhere in chains. Men are naturally social beings and equal, but everywhere they are in conflict and unequal. Mankind is benevolent and angelic, but is everywhere alienated from its true self. No vision of human potential could be further from the realities of the sons and daughters of Adam, confused in their hearts between right and wrong, whose exile is the reflection of their disobedient wills.

Just as religious gnosticism sees evil as a flaw in the cosmic creation, so secular gnosticism sees evil as a flaw in the social cosmos, as a force external to humanity itself. For the secular gnostics of the socialist Left, this flaw in the cosmos is private property. It is private property that creates alienation and inequality, irrationality and social conflict, and condemns humanity to perpetual exile from its own freedom. To set mankind on the path back to an earthly paradise, it is only necessary to abolish property. In this messianic vision, redemption does not lie in the fulfillment of moral covenants and the adherence to law, but in the abolition and "transcendence" of both. Its path is not disclosed by divine grace but by a human reason that is, in fact, not reason at all, but a mysticism of liberation. This mysticism is at the heart of every movement that seeks a revolutionary transformation of the world we know.

In this revolutionary mysticism, the messianic liberator is imprisoned in capitalist darkness; the liberator is an agent without property, that is in society but not of it; a force that is revolutionary because its revolt is not against the particular injustices of man's social existence, but the injustice of the existence itself. The messianic force is a class of people dispersed among the nations, but not of the nations, who in lifting the yoke of their own oppression will lift the yoke of all.

In socialist theology, this class is the proletariat, the Chosen People of the Marxist faith. The proletariat, according to Marx, is a class "which has a universal character by reason of the universality of its sufferings, and which does not lay claim to any specific rights because the injustice to which it is subjected is not particular but general. . . . It cannot liberate itself without breaking free from all the other classes of society and thereby liberating them also. . . . It stands for the total ruin of man, and can recover itself only by his total redemption."[18]

Here we see the mystical core of the Marxist faith, and of all the faiths of the revolutionary Left: a class representing the "total ruin of man" will bring about the "total redemption" of man. This is a logical absurdity. But, as gnostic heresy, it is theologically precise: light from darkness.

The analytically specific "proletariat" has been replaced in the liberation theology of the contemporary Left by the generic "poor" and "Third World oppressed," by exploited races and downtrodden genders. But the formula has not changed. From total ruin, redemption; from oppression, liberation; from evil, good. From the fallen children of Adam and Eve, self-creating gods.

In his notorious preface to Frantz Fanon's *The Wretched of the Earth,* the French radical Jean-Paul Sartre extols the violent path of revolutionary redemption that will restore humanity to its paradise lost: "This irrepressible violence is neither sound and fury, nor the resurrection of savage instincts, nor even the effect of resentment: it is man recreating himself. . . . The native cures himself of colonial neurosis by thrusting out the settler through force of arms. When his rage boils over, he rediscovers his lost innocence and he comes to know himself in that he himself creates his self."

You shall be as God.

Here we see the sinister, seductive spell of the gnostic illusion, and its *tikkun olam:* You, Nathan of Gaza, shall no longer be a youthful divinity student, but a prophet, a "holy lamp" unto the nations; and you, Shabbtai Zvi, shall no longer be a misfit and outcast, but a messiah. The gnostic doctrines of Nathan of Gaza and Karl Marx are doctrines of self-loathing and self-exaltation, the enthronement of man in general and of mankind's self-anointed redeemers in particular. To eat from the tree of radical theory will make you gods. This is the socialist delusion, the intoxicating fantasy that makes the socially alienated into political saviors: not the compassion of angels, but the arrogance of the Serpent—the belief that revolutionary ideas can confer the power of self-creation, the power of gods.

This is what makes radicals so dangerous and destructive. Since (for the revolutionary) the End of Days is at hand, the rejection of the law, of the old prohibitions, is the sign of election. The benediction of all revolutionaries is "To Him Who Allows the Forbidden." Redemption through sin. Thus Sartre: "When the peasant takes a gun in his hands, the old myths grow dim and the prohibitions are one by one forgotten. The rebel's weapon is the proof of his humanity. . . . to shoot down a European is to kill two birds with one stone, to destroy an oppressor and the man he oppresses at the same time: there remain a dead man, and a free man. . . ." Out of darkness, light.

Here we see the murderous, dehumanizing passion of the Left in all its gnostic splendor. Here is the voice of Pol Pot ordering the extermination of educated Cambodians in order that Cambodia might be free of oppressive culture. Here is the voice of Winnie Mandela praising the necklacing of black South Africans burned alive in order that South Africa might be liberated. Here is the voice of Marx proclaiming the emancipation of the Jews through the emancipation of mankind from Judaism itself.

Marx was indeed the prototype of the radical "non-Jewish Jew," much as my parents and I were, as we marched down Eighth Avenue in that May Day parade when I was nine. We were Jews who had turned our backs on Judaism, but who belonged to no other real community or place. We were in America, but not of it. We had embraced a cause that set us against it. We had puffed ourselves up into thinking we were saviors of humanity, but we did not really identify ourselves with any particular part of the humanity we intended to save. If we had the courage to be truthful, in fact, we would have admitted that, in our own eyes, like Shabbtai Zvi, we were really nothing at all. We had taken up a messianic cause in behalf of all humanity, especially black and poor humanity, and the Third World's oppressed. But we had no cause that was our own. Those we championed hated us as Jews, as middle-class people who had made a modest success, and as Americans too.

The international socialist creed that Marx invented is a creed of hate and self-hate. The solution that Marxism proposes to the Jewish "problem" is to eliminate the system that "creates" the Jew. Judaism is only the symptom of a more extensive evil that must be eradicated: capitalism. Jews are only symbols of a more pervasive enemy that must be destroyed: capitalists. In the politics of the Left, racist hatred is directed not only against Jewish capitalists but against all capitalists; not only against capitalists, but against anyone who is not poor, and who is white; and ultimately against western civilization itself. The socialist revolution is anti-Semitism elevated to a global principle.[19] From darkness, light.

A former radical, a heretic and stranger, what I have learned through my own exile is this: respect for the boundaries between the profane and the holy, between man and God; distrust of the false prophets of a *tikkun olam*. Marxism and liberation theology are satanic creeds. There can be no return from our exile by any path other than the moral law; no redemption that takes us beyond the boundaries of who and what we are.

CHAPTER FOUR

THE MEANING OF
LEFT AND RIGHT

*The Western world was the seat of freedom until
another, more Western, was discovered; and that
other will be probably its asylum when it is hunted
down in every other part.*

—Edmund Burke

IN A SPEECH TO A MEETING OF "DEMOCRATIC RUSSIA,"
delivered in Moscow on June 1, 1991, a year after the dissolution of the
Soviet Union, Boris Yeltsin described the catastrophe that had befallen
his nation: "Our country has not been lucky. It was decided to carry out
this Marxist experiment on us. It has simply pushed us off the path the
world's civilized countries have taken. . . . In the end, we proved that
there is no place for this idea."

For the Left outside the former Soviet Union, this verdict is still inconceivable. To embrace it would be to make peace with the enemy, the

democracies of the West. It would mean the dissolution of its own identity as a Left. Indeed, what is troubling to the community of the Left is not the catastrophe of Soviet socialism so much as the idea that this history should culminate in disenchantment with the utopian project. What the Left cannot face is the prospect that an understanding of this century of revolutionary grief should lead, finally, to *conservative* conclusions: to reconciliation to the finite parameters of the human condition—the unavoidable conflicts and inevitable insufficiencies that make up ordinary social unhappiness. In other words, acceptance of who and what we are.

What troubles the radical heart, finally, is the sense of limits that such understanding provokes. To be a revolutionary, by contrast, is to live with a sense of social horizons that are literally without end.

To be sure, large contingents of the Left are now prepared to concede a great deal that previously would have been unthinkable to them: the failure of Marxism, the evils of Communism, the taint that socialism has incurred by its genetic involvement with both. But even leftists who concede as much still do not want to give up the noble ambitions behind the tarnished hope. They will give up the socialist past but not the socialist future; they will distance themselves from the totalitarian temptation while continuing to embrace the radical cause.

It is not giving up the socialist Idea that haunts today's progressives so much as it is conceding the argument to their lifelong opponents. It is the thought of becoming one of *them* that is repellent—not just a chastened missionary of the radical cause but a *counterrevolutionary* of the Right. This is the term of surrender that sticks in their throats, the nightmare vision that troubles their sleep and makes them hold on to their broken faith. To abandon a lifetime's loyalties, to become a *conservative*—where is the romance in that? What would remain of their progressive hopes, their desire for justice, their sense of themselves as a chosen vanguard, if they were to take this unthinkable step?

What remains then of the division between Left and Right that has so defined our political lives? The terms are more than just a vestigial homage to 1789. They identify historical attitudes and traditions, the parties that have contended over the fate of modernity ever since. They recall the scars of battles won and lost, of aspirations realized and deferred. It is through them that we locate our historical forebears in the struggles for justice and human freedom, and it is through their causes that we assess our humanity and measure who we are.

Or have, until now. For with the fall of Communism, we have reached a turning point in our collective lives. The history of revolutionary modernity—this narrative through which we have traditionally located our social selves—has finally come to a close. The tearing down of the Berlin Wall marked the end of the modern epoch as surely as the fall of the Bastille marked its beginning two centuries ago. Like all endings, this changes our understanding of what went before.

It is now impossible to console ourselves any longer with the illusion that socialism might have worked if only this path or that panacea had been tried. In our lifetime, the revolutions of the Left have created despotisms and oppressions that dwarf all others on human record. Nonetheless, to the diehards of the radical culture, "Left" still evokes the idealism of a "progressive" cause, while "Right" remains synonymous with social reaction. It is time for a change in our understanding of the terms themselves.

In what sense can a bankrupt idea be called "progressive"? For two centuries, the socialist idea—the future promise that justifies the present sacrifice—has functioned as a blank check for the violence and injustice associated with efforts to achieve it. If the "experiments" have failed—so go the apologies for the Left—the intentions that launched them were idealistic and noble. But it is no longer really possible to invoke the socialist fantasy to justify the assaults on societies that, whatever their faults, were less oppressive than the revolutionary "solutions" that followed their demise. The divisive crusades of the Left and its failed "experiments" must be seen now for what they are: bloody exercises in civil nihilism; violent pursuits of empty hopes; revolutionary *actes gratuites* that were doomed to fail from the start.

Historical perspective imposes on us a new standard of judgment. Because they were doomed from their origin and destructive by design, these revolutionary gestures now stand condemned by morality and justice *in their conception* and not merely in their result. If there was a "party of humanity" in the civil wars that the Left's ambitions provoked in the past, it was on the other side of the political barricades. In these battles, the enlightened parties were those who defended democratic process and civil order against the greater barbarism that we now know for certain the radical future entailed.

The term "counterrevolutionary," which leftists find so difficult to digest, is really a litmus of their failure to understand the history they have lived. In our time, 100 million people have been slaughtered in the revolutions of the Left with no positive result, while millions more have been buried alive. Beyond the iron curtains of the socialist empires, whole cultures were desecrated, civilizations destroyed and generations deprived of the barest essentials of a tolerable life. Yet the epithet "counterrevolutionary" still strikes progressives, who supported these empires, as a term of opprobrium and moral disgrace. What this record shows, on the contrary, is that "counterrevolution" is a name for moral sanity and human decency, a term for resistance to the epic depredations of dreamers like them.

The very word "counterrevolutionary" was invented by the virtuous terrorists of the French Revolution to stigmatize their opponents on the way to the guillotine. The first counterrevolutionaries were in fact the very people in whose name the revolution had triumphed, the Catholic peasants of the Vendée. A quarter of a million such enemies of the radical future were slaughtered in the Jacobin Terror of the revolutionary Year II. The peasants of the Vendée were not opposed to the changes of 1789—the constitutional reforms of the monarchy, the Declaration of the Rights of Man, the enfranchisement of the Third Estate—but to the revolutionary dictatorship that followed. It was the new liberated order, the Republic of Virtue and the Cult of Reason (and the Reign of Terror required to make its citizens virtuous and reasonable), that inspired their resistance and made them *counter*revolutionary.

Abroad, the chief apostle of the counterrevolution was the English liberal Edmund Burke. Burke was not an opponent of political reform or the establishment of a republic, but of the radical attempt to transform society, to recreate it *de novo*. It is this *totalitarian* ambition—to reject the past and remake humanity—that has triggered the opposition of counterrevolutionaries ever since.

The Leninist creators of the Soviet Union were self-conscious heirs of the Jacobin vanguard who saw in their revolutionary usurpation an effort to complete the transformation that Robespierre had only begun. In exterminating the "enemies of the people," the Leninists found the term "counterrevolutionary" an indispensable weapon. They used it first to discredit the liberals who opposed their October coup against the democracy that had replaced the czarist regime. They applied it then to their Menshevik rivals, to anarchists, Kronstadters, Oppositionists, Trotskyists, Bukharinites, even anti-Stalin Stalinists and, ultimately, to every recalcitrant soul who stood in the path of their revolutionary dreams. Like their Jacobin heroes, the Leninists also created an empire that was Napoleonic in scope. But seventy years after the creation, its subjects rose en masse, in the largest counterrevolution in human history, to put an end to the Marxist epoch.

Nearly two hundred years earlier, the reactionary philosopher Joseph de Maistre quarreled with the term the Jacobins had applied to their political opponents. "The re-establishment of the monarchy, which is called *Counter-revolution*," he wrote in 1797, "will not be a *contrary revolution*, but the *contrary of the Revolution*."[1] Reactionaries like Maistre were not supporters of 1789, but royalist defenders of the *ancien régime*. They were not proponents of a different kind of revolution (a *counter* revolution). They were *contrary* to the revolution against the absolute monarch; they were supporters of the *status quo ante*, the old order as it was before the flood.

Bearing this in mind, look again at the pivotal events of 1989 and 1990. The mass upheavals in the Soviet satellites and the dramatic finale in Moscow itself were not the contrary of the revolution of 1917, but a true counter*revolution*. They aspired not to the restoration of the old czarist regime, but to a new democratic order. The future they invoked was an antithesis of the one the Leninists had imposed, and this antithesis was precisely that revolutionary future—bourgeois and democratic, capitalist and individualist—whose paradigm Burke himself had defended when it was established in America in 1776.

Looking back on the two-hundred-year history now past, we can see that it is not simply a unitary conflict between revolution and *ancien régime* (the paradigm in which counterrevolution *would* be synonymous with reaction, revolution with social progress). It is the conflict of two distinct revolutionary traditions. The struggle that has shaped our age has not been between the old order and the new revolution, but between two revolutionary paths to the modern world, two different paradigms of the European Enlightenment that took root, respectively, in America and France.

The Cold War is often presented as a power struggle with no particular historical dimension. But it is more accurately seen as the climactic phase of the conflict between these contending traditions. The radical ethos of the French Revolution became the wellspring of a socialist revolt against bourgeois order that culminated in the creation of the Soviet empire. On the other hand, the libertarian ethos of the American Revolution inspired the conservative opponents of the Soviet tyranny, a *counter*revolution based on individual rights, free markets and democratic constitutions. The revolutionary societies that followed this path formed an alliance of free nations confronting the Soviet empire, an alliance whose triumph in the Cold War has now brought the totalitarian era to a close.

Those on the Left who do not want to face the implications of their historic defeat prefer to be puzzled by what are otherwise straightforward events. The triumph of the Right in this riptide of freedom is so unthinkable to them that they speak of the counterrevolutions in the Eastern bloc as though they were an enigma impenetrable to understanding. Because the democrats in the Soviet Union are called "radicals" and the Communists are called "conservatives," because the advocates of capitalism in Eastern Europe are called "Left" and the die-hard socialists "Right," they conclude that we have arrived at a new "end of ideology."

In their perspective, the very concepts of Left and Right have lost their meaning, and a new political vocabulary is required to name the alternatives we face.

But is it? Only if one insists on viewing this history through the political prism of the radical tradition. Only if one wants to avoid a reckoning with the socialist defeat, to preserve the ideological framework of the political Left. Only if one wants to preserve the traditional sense of a radical past in the hope of one day reviving the sense of a radical future.

If we reject this reasoning, however, and recognize the existence of two traditions in conflict, the difficulty vanishes. When these two traditions confront each other across the Iron Curtain created by their historic conflict, Left and Right become inverse images. Within the Soviet bloc, "Left" signifies *counter*revolution—capitalism, liberalism, democracy; "Right" means the *contrary* of the revolution—defense of the conservative status quo (the Marxist dictatorship, communism, socialism). In the West, it is just the opposite: the status quo of the revolution, defended by "conservatives" of the Right, is liberal, democratic and free.

In short, once we leave the swamps of the leftist worldview, the confusion of terminologies becomes clarity itself. To be conservative within a revolutionary tradition simply means to conserve the paradigm peculiar to that revolution. To be conservative in the context of the democratic West means to preserve the liberal, individualist and free-market framework that is its historic achievement and to act on the nonutopian premises that are its philosophical foundation.

WHAT DOES IT mean in this post-Communist era to be Left within the liberal framework of the West? That is the real question posed by this historic upheaval and its political crossroads. For two hundred years, the leftist counterrevolution against liberal democracy has meant permanent war against bourgeois society—against the culture of individual rights and political pluralism, against the private property foundations of the liberal state. To have been on the left is to have been at war with the only democratic and free societies the world has ever known. It has been a war conducted in the name of ideals that cannot be implemented and a future that cannot work, and has brought misery and oppression of incalculable dimensions to uncountable millions.

Leftists will object. They do not want to be put in the same political bed with Leninists and Marxists and other totalitarians—especially now that the world has repudiated them. Now these leftists insist that they are *democratic* socialists (making the assumption that there is a real-world meaning to this self-validating phrase).[2] Or they will call themselves "populists" and "egalitarians," as though there were some other way than socialist *diktat* to legislate their agendas.

It is true, of course, that since the collapse of the Soviet economies, many "democratic socialists" are eager to concede that markets cannot be so easily discarded without incurring consequences that are unacceptable. On occasion, they even allow themselves to express the thought (previously unthinkable) that perhaps, in the end, "socialism" can only be a term for a more humane form of the capitalist enterprise. Sometimes of late, they have seemed willing to claim any reform—the establishment of unions or a minimum wage—as victories for "socialist" ideas. The very minimalism of this position is revealing. There remains something so visceral in their identification with the socialist cause, so passionate in their belief in a remade world, that they are unable to take the honorable course—to admit they were wrong, to give up the radical ghost, and to redefine themselves as advocates of capitalist reform. Instead, they insist (and with the same old smugness) that socialism remains the name of their desire.

In the end, the concessions these leftists are ready to make now seem less a gesture of self-understanding than a strategy for avoiding further defeat. Consider the new name they have adopted to signal their willingness to modify the old ideal of a general plan: *market socialism*. Whole libraries were written by social democrats to prove that market economy is the root of our afflictions—a reifying, alienating, dehumanizing incubus on the social life of mankind. Yet, on the basis virtually of a single chapter in a solitary book on the economics of "feasible socialism,"[3] they have rushed to enlist the market as a remedy for the ills of socialism, now that its bankruptcy is apparent to all. How readily they now appropriate an institution they condemned when the life chances of millions hung in the balance.

These democratic socialists are willing to make concessions if only they do not have to give up anything that really matters. They are ready, now, to acknowledge the necessity of the market as the minimal price they must pay to remain part of any rational discourse. But their contrition does not appear to go further than that. Otherwise, why continue to call themselves "socialists"? Why cling to an identity and attitude so thoroughly disgraced? Why remain in the political company of unrepentant radicals who are still "Marxists" and still recklessly committed to agendas about which they, themselves, claim to have had second thoughts? The answer can only lie in the beliefs they have *not* given up, which they still share in common with their erstwhile comrades, and which are at the heart of the tradition they still call their own. These are the passions that even now thrill their blood, the faith in which they will always feel at home.

WHAT DOES IT mean to hold on to this faith, to be radically Left within the political tradition of the liberal West? This Left, whose project has culminated in human calamity beyond comprehension, began with the famous passage in Rousseau's *Discourse on the Origin and Foundations of Inequality* in which he first articulated the radical myth of social creation:

> The first man, who after enclosing a piece of ground, took it into his head to say, *this is mine,* and found people simple enough to believe him, was the real founder of civil society.

To which Rousseau exclaims, in words that reverberate through the tragedies of our time: *"How many crimes, how many wars, how many murders, how many misfortunes and horrors, would that man have saved the human species, who pulling up the stakes or filling up the ditches should have cried to his fellows: Beware of listening to this impostor; you are lost, if you forget that the fruits of the earth belong equally to us all, and the earth itself to nobody!"*

For the next two centuries, this idea served as inspiration for the radical onslaught against liberal democracy in the West. Indeed, the charge that private property corrupted humanity became the basic proposition of all political Lefts, that is of all attempts to construct a radical future in which "socially created" evils, like inequality and injustice, would be relegated to the museum of human antiquities.

Two centuries later, the relentless unraveling of these socialist schemes has shifted the onus of Rousseau's question. Now we must ask: *How many crimes, how many wars, how many murders, how many misfortunes and horrors, would the human species have been spared, had the world not listened to this radical impostor, when he assaulted private property, the very foundation of liberty, while invoking the unlimited powers of the state to make men virtuous and equal?*

It is *this* question and *this* recognition that mark the dividing line between Left and Right. For Rousseau, as for the radicals who followed him, "democratic" and otherwise, "society" is the root of human oppression: "Man was born free, yet is everywhere in chains." The radical's goal everywhere is a transformation of society that will liberate the "authentic" human self and bring about the recovery of natural innocence. That will restore the harmonious human community allegedly lost, that was first corrupted and then suppressed by private property and its state. But the history of socialism has now shown (as for two hundred years conservatives warned it would) that humanity liberated from the claims of property and from the disciplines of the market, from religious constraint and from the rule of law—humanity governed by its general will—is a monster of barbarism and atavistic evil.

For the counterrevolution of the Right, the truth revealed about humanity in society is exactly the opposite of the Rousseauian claim: Man is not born free, but helpless and dependent, and then a slave to his unruly passions. Society is not nature's corrupter, but a civilizing, humanizing force. "What is government," an American founder wrote, "but a reflection on human nature?" And: "If men were angels, there would be no need for government." It is only the civilizing limits of the social contract that can liberate the antisocial creatures of nature into the constitutive orders of productive and communal life.

This is the pragmatic realism that informs the American paradigm and creates the conservative attitude. Its argument is summarized in Madison's celebrated discussion of political factions in *The Federalist,* No. 10. The social problems that egalitarians of the Left propose to eradicate are finally the problems of Madisonian "faction," the Eighteenth-Century rubric for race, class and other social divisions. In devising a countersolution to these problems, therefore, *The Federalist,* No. 10 also defines a conservative paradigm:

- There are two methods of curing the mischiefs of faction: the one by removing its *causes;* the other, by controlling its *effects.*
- There are again two methods of removing the *causes* of faction: the one, by destroying the liberty which is essential to its existence; the other by giving to every citizen the same opinions, the same passions, and the same interests. [emphasis added]

In this passage, the history of the last two centuries—the struggle between Left and Right over the future of the liberal state—is distilled in two propositions.

As between the two prescriptions for curing the mischiefs of faction, the conservative takes the path of realism and attempts to control its effects. The radical, by contrast, chooses the removal of causes—the very method eschewed by the American Founders because it leads, inexorably, to the destruction of liberty. Throughout the modern era, the radical has defined himself by his determination to remove the root *causes* of human faction, in order to eliminate suffering and oppression. By contrast, the conservative recognizes the impossibility of such a quest, and is content, instead, to manage the conflicts to contain the *effects* of evils that are integral to our humanity and cannot be erased. Such accommodation to reality is anathema to the radical spirit.

In the radical impulse to redeem humanity, the conservative recognizes a primal threat to human liberty. The determination to eradicate the causes of social conflict, to make society one and indivisible is nothing less than the totalitarian ambition. The ambition is to change human nature by political means. It is the promise (in Rousseau's revealing formulation) *"to force men to be free."*

Writing before the French Revolution and the advent of the modern Left, Madison was skeptical that any social faction would actually attempt to control the consciousness of others in order to create a unity of interest and equality of condition among all. To Madison such a program was self-evidently impractical. The diversity of human opinion was a fact of nature. As long as humanity was free, its opinions would never be unified. Human faculties and talents were diverse and different from birth. From these differences flowed inequalities that were inevitable, including the inequality of property in which human energies and talents were ultimately invested. In protecting the efforts of the individuals in whom they are vested, property rights are the foundation of human rights, the indispensable shield of human diversity.

It is the rights of property—and (behind them) the rights of diverse and unequal individuals—that form the insuperable obstacle to the socialist desires: equality, unity, the harmony of human interests. As Madison expressed these ideas:

> From the protection of different and unequal faculties of acquiring property, the possession of different degrees and kinds of property immediately results; and from the influence of these on the sentiments and views of the respective proprietors ensues a division of the society into different interests and parties.

But it is the unity of interest and the equality of condition—objectives that were for Madison impossible to achieve—that are the all-consuming goals of the modern Left. To suppress human nature and human difference is, in essence, the Left's utopian ambition—an ambition that requires the totalitarian state.

Ever since the French Revolution, radical "equality" and conservative "liberty" have opposed each other as the defining agendas of Left and

Right. For radicals, freedom is the *power* to redefine human destiny and has invariably meant the surrender of individual autonomy to the radical project, to collective truth and the "progressive" idea. For conservatives, in contrast, liberty is *relief* for the individual from collective power. It is secured by "negative rights," by *limits* to government. Liberty is made possible by the civilizing bonds of social order, and restraints on the coercive power of civil authority.

The conservative goal is democratic, but it is also circumspect and modest (and so, deeply unsatisfying to the radical soul). Better to live with some injustices than, by seeking perfect justice, create a world with none. This is the political caution that has been etched in blood on the historical ledger of the last two hundred years. It is the lesson the Left refuses to learn. It is this refusal that makes radicals the dangerous reactionaries of the postmodern world.

This very denial of history, however, also creates the political mask that allows leftists to appear as social reformers. Refusing to acknowledge any connection to the destructive consequences of their radical faith, the Left has been able to hijack the vocabulary of political discourse, to appropriate the terms "democratic" and "progressive," and now even "liberal" and "market," and to frame its agendas in the misleading imagery of "social justice."[4] The Left flies under permanently false colors. It is neither liberal nor progressive, and the justice it promises is achievable only through political coercion and totalitarian terror.

Despite the Left's surface adjustment to historical realities in the post-Communist era, the character of its project remains stubbornly the same. This project, as before, is antithetic to the American paradigm and the stoic realism in which its liberties are grounded. The opposition is so fundamental that even those left-wing revisionists who have accepted a part of the democratic achievement, and call themselves "democratic socialists," reveal a profound and dedicated hostility to the American founding and its political truths.

This deep-seated enmity to the American framework is nowhere better illustrated than in the last work of Michael Harrington, America's most articulate spokesman for a "democratic" Left. Harrington wrestled all his life with the perplexing legacies of his political commitment, and his works record a dogged if doomed effort to rescue radical theory from its antidemocratic course. The last chapter in this effort, completed in 1989 while the author was ill with cancer, appeared posthumously under the title *Socialism: Past and Future.* Written in the shadow of Communist collapse, it was an attempt to reassert the socialist claim to be "the hope for human freedom and justice."

Like generations of socialists before him, Harrington's ideological point of departure was the French Revolution.[5] Like them, he regarded the Revolution as a compromised triumph because it had achieved equality only in the political sphere. To "complete" the Revolution by extending the principle of equality into the economic realm was the socialist task. Until this was accomplished, humanity would not be free.

> The [bourgeois revolution] opened up *possibilities* of freedom and justice, not inevitabilities. After all, the rulers of the system were, more often than not, horrified by the unintended potential of their own magnificent accomplishment. They were terrified that civil rights for the people. . . . would mean an end of property rights for the elite.[6]

To protect their privilege, these ruling classes contrived to thwart the popular will, to prevent the people from acting on their common interests. According to Harrington, the very pinnacle of this cynicism was reached by the Founding Fathers when they devised the keystone of the American paradigm. "All this was theorized," he wrote, "with stunning clarity in the *Tenth Federalist Paper* of James Madison, in one of the greatest defenses of human manipulation in the history of political theory."

In other words, the truly revolutionary formulation of *The Federalist,* No. 10, the division of powers implemented in the Constitution and, ever since, the great bulwark of American freedom, is the principle condemned by Harrington as a cynically contrived *obstacle* to freedom, to the direct expression of the people's will. Madison's central premise that economic inequality originates in human nature and cannot be eliminated without abolishing liberty itself is, thus, cavalierly dismissed. For Harrington, American democracy is only "bourgeois democracy," the halfway democracy allowed by the ruling class to protect its wealth. For Harrington, the task of the "democratic" socialist revolution is, still, to destroy this obstacle to radical leveling, and along with it, the property rights that are freedom's most fundamental guarantee. The final word of America's most flexible social democrat, in short, is only the latest radical declaration of war on the American idea, on its Madisonian framework and its liberal conception of human freedom. So consistent, through all these two hundred years of revolutionary tragedy, has the radical assault remained.

In understanding the passionate depths of the radical assault, it is instructive to confront Harrington's intellectual inertia with the second thoughts of ex-Communists in Eastern Europe. Unlike Harrington, their hands-on experience with socialist economy caused them to abandon the false Marxist consciousness that condemned markets as instruments of alienation and exploitation. Instead, they recognized private property and the market as the irreplaceable engines of material prosperity and technical progress for the whole of society, a development as important for human welfare as the invention of civilization itself.

By contrast, Harrington's views remain, to the end, mired in the vulgar simplicities of the Marxist model. Despite his grudging recognition of the market's capacity "to coordinate an extraordinary range of human desires," it remained for him as "pernicious" a construct as for Marx himself—"a mechanism for maximizing profits rather than human needs." As though "desire" and "need" were discrete, and human satisfactions were not promoted and served by efficient production for consumer markets. In insinuating that production for profit is antithetical to production for need, socialists like Harrington reinforce the very Marxist formulas that created the endless poverty and boundless tyranny of the Soviet world. It is this above all, and despite their disavowals, that makes them complicit in the tragedies of the socialist epoch that is now past, and dangerous guides to the social future.

TO BE A LEFTIST, then, is to be at war with the two most profoundly liberating achievements of modern history: the liberal state and the liberal economy. These are the twin pillars of what Hayek called the Great Society, which he described as a spontaneous, "extended order of human cooperation."[7] Such a society is not the product of vanguard schemes like the socialist design, but of a long process of adjustments to reality that eventually lead to more productive and humane institutions and rules. Capitalist democracy (a system as flawed as humanity is flawed) is, in this view, the highest stage of social evolution.

In contrast, socialism belongs to the dark, prehistory of mankind. In the words of Hayek, it is "a re-assertion of that tribal ethics whose gradual weakening . . . made an approach to [civilized market societies] possible."[8] Socialism belongs to a social stage based on the simple economy of small groups, a stage that had to be overcome in order to realize the great wealth-making potential of the market system. Far from being a progressive conception, the socialist ethic is atavistic and represents the primitive morality of preindustrial formations: the clan and the tribe. This is why its current incarnation takes the form of "identity politics," the latest revolt against bourgeois individualism and freedom. Modern radicalism is the return of the repressed. Its values—equality, cooperation, unity—are the survival codes of small, vulnerable groups with knowable goals and shared interests. But the morality of tribal communities is self-defeating and disastrous when applied to complex economies, dependent on factors of production that are geographically dispersed and on trade exchanges that are transnational in scope. In the context of a modern extended economic order, where goals are not shared, where market prices encapsulate knowledge beyond the capacity of a central authority and in situations so complex that no planner can rationally allocate economic tasks, the socialist agenda and its tribal ethos produce social atavisms—the paternalistic politics, fratricidal nationalisms and economic despotisms universally characteristic of socialist states.

Socialist morality is a seductive illusion. Because it does not rest on real-world assumptions, the socialist ethic, if put into practice, would threaten to undermine the life basis of vast communities of present-day humanity and to impoverish much of the rest.

Far from being progressive, the Left's demands for "social justice," if realized, would destroy the very basis of social wealth (as it has in the former regions of the Soviet bloc). In the modern world, competition is not the contrary of cooperation, but the form that cooperation must take in order to coordinate the activities of millions of people unknown to each other, pursuing goals that are not common and cannot be shared. The profit motive is the engine of wealth not only for the rich but for the poor as well. In the real world, the attempt to plan economic systems produces inefficiency and waste; the attempt to redistribute wealth diminishes well-being and individual liberty; the attempt to unify society crushes its freedom; the ambition to make people equal creates new forms of tyranny and submerges human individuality in totalitarian designs.

For a long time, the tribal ethos of socialism was concealed in the universalist membrane of the Marxist movement and the liberationist impulse of its proletarian myth. But the collapse of Communism has disintegrated the Marxist idea and fragmented the culture of the international Left. The result is a proliferation of post-Marxian theories and identity politics that no longer base themselves on the universalist category of economic class but on the particularist identities of gender, ethnicity and race. The class struggle has been replaced by status conflict; the universalist idea, by quasi-fascist doctrines of racial solidarity, group rights and antiliberal political agendas.

These agendas are still inspired by the essential radical theme. They share the Rousseauian desire to redefine and repossess the world in terms of a collective idea of self, to regenerate the lost paradise of human beginnings, and to unify alienated society under the redemptive aegis of a tribal will. "An atavistic longing after the life of the noble savage," as Hayek has written, "is the main source of the collectivist tradition."

Thus, the post-Marxian Left has begun its career by launching an all-out assault on the third great achievement of modern history, the liberal community itself. This community, whose paradigm is America, is founded in a universal compact that transcends tribal identities and the multicultural particularisms of blood and soil. "No nation before ever made diversity itself a source of national identity and unity," a historian has written, "a nation created by people of all classes and ethnicities, immigrating from all over the world."[9] America is the unique crystallization of an idea of nationality residing in a shared commitment to universal principles and pluralistic values. This creed is the culmination of an evolution that extends backward in time to Jerusalem, and Athens, and Rome. It encapsulates lessons that were accumulated through practice and acquired by faith, that are inscribed in the teachings of sacred tradition and the institutions of secular law. These traditions (as it happens, Judaeo-Christian traditions) and these institutions (in fact, bourgeois-democratic institutions) have led us to the truths that are self-evident, and on which our freedom finally depends.

CHAPTER FIVE

A RADICAL HOLOCAUST

Everyone who preached free love in the Sixties is responsible for AIDS. . . . This idea that it was somehow an accident, a microbe that sort of fell from heaven—absurd. We must face what we did.

—Camille Paglia

A SPECTER IS HAUNTING THE AMERICAN UNIVERSITY, THE last refuge of the Marxist left. It is the specter of "queer theory," the latest version of the radical "identity politics" that have replaced economic struggles in the schema of revolution. Amid the din and clatter of utopias crashing messily to earth, true believers once again are burnishing the agendas of social transformation. This time it is no longer as class warriors, however, but as aggrieved partisans of oppressed races, genders and sexes. "As work is to Marxism, sexuality is to feminism," proclaims a leading "theoretician" of the new radical era,[1] in a logically absurd call to overthrow gender categories and the "patriarchal" order. In parallel lock-step, black radicals disparage assimilation into the "dominant white culture," preferring liberation into a society of "Afro-centric" values instead.[2]

Gay radicals aspire to no less. "Queer politics is no longer content to carve out a buffer zone for a minoritized and protected subculture," an academic manifesto titled "Fear of a Queer Planet" declares.[3] Its goal is "to challenge the pervasive and often invisible hetero-normativity of modern societies," by which the author means the oppressive structure of normality that divides humanity into two sexes. The same idea was expressed without the academic obscurantism by a writer in the *Village Voice:* "It isn't enough to become parallel to straights. We want to obliterate such dichotomies altogether."

Oppressor and oppressed, victimizer and victim—these dichotomies are the indispensable categories of radical thought. The radical worldview divides humanity into the oppressed who suffer as the objects of the historical process and the oppressors who inflict the process on everyone else. Power is always systemic, always an alien force.[4] For the traditional Marxist, the enemy system that organizes and distributes power is capitalism; for the radical feminist, it is patriarchy; and for the queer theorist, it is "hetero-normativity." Liberation can only lie in the annihilation of the system that creates the antagonism. Liberation is conceived not as a modification or even a reversal of traditional order, but its transcendence. For the Marxist radical, the liberated future is the classless society; for the queer radical, it is the genderless planet.

From this perspective of revolution, sexual dichotomies are already being erased in liberated zones throughout the popular culture. A *San Francisco Chronicle* writer swept up in this cultural wave waxed messianic when reviewing a Michael Jackson video, which was seen by half a billion youngsters across the globe: "The refrain in the *Black and White* video is 'It doesn't matter if you're black or white.' Most riveting is a computer-enhanced segment where a person changes ethnicity and sex in rapid succession. . . . In a world threatened by racial tensions and overpopulation, the survival instinct could summon a new human, one who has no single race and who, by being . . . androgynous, is less subject to the procreative urge." This outburst of millennial enthusiasm prompted a wry observation from the novelist Saul Bellow: "The idea is to clobber everything that used to be accepted as given, fixed, irremediable." Clobbering the irremediable is the essential aim of the radical assault. In the words of the above-cited manifesto, the revolutionary task is "to confront . . . modern culture with its worst nightmare, a queer planet."

To the queer theorist, all identities, gay and straight, are the product of the socially imposed ideal—hetero-normativity—which structures the system of oppression. For the new revolutionaries, the enemy is no longer a ruling class or a hegemonic race or even a dominant gender, but the sexual order of nature itself. As the author of "Fear of a Queer Planet" explains, queerness opposes "not just the normal behavior of the social, but the idea of normal behavior." Oppression lies in the very *idea* of the normal, the fixed order that arrays humanity into two complementary, procreating sexes. It is the gender-patriarchy system through which heterosexual males oppress their victims: women and gays. In Catharine MacKinnon's preposterous formulation, "Women and men are divided by gender, made into the sexes as we know them, by the social requirements of its dominant form, heterosexuality, which institutionalizes male sexual dominance and female sexual submission."[5] In other words, it is not nature but "society" that creates two sexes, and does so in order that one might dominate the other. The task of the sexual revolutionary is to overthrow the norm that structures this oppression.

Queer revolution is thus the ultimate subversive project. It proclaims not only the death of society's God, but of nature's law—the very idea of a reality beyond the control of human will. For these revolutionaries, not even biology constrains human possibility or limits human hope. Theirs is the consummate Nieztschean fantasy: a world in which humanity *is* God. On this brave new horizon, mankind can finally realize its potential as a self-creating species able to defy even its own sexual gravity. The transformed future will give birth not just to a "new man" and "new woman," but to a new revolutionary people, no longer male and female, but queer. "Queer" is the Promethean category of the contemporary left, the triumph of the revolutionary subject over history and nature, the postmodern vision of a brave new world.

In its queer formulation, the radical project has reached its outer limit, realizing what the young Marx might have called its "species-essence." For the concept of queer is really the modern revolutionary idea in crystalline form. It is the cry of the Unhappy Consciousness: *That which is normal oppresses me.*

To others, the normal institutional orders of democracy appear as liberating structures in whose environment individuals can achieve, breathe free, and realize their desires, without falling into anarchy or chaos. It is the Hobbesian dilemma resolved: liberty ordered by the rule of law, and economy maintained by market constraints. To the alienated radical, however, democracy is only a more deceptive form of oppression. It is oppressive *because* of the very freedoms it permits; because it *appears* to be free while failing to live up to radical expectations. In the words of Herbert Marcuse, a theorist of the New Left, liberal capitalism is a system of "repressive tolerance."

In this view, the institutional forms of capitalist democracies are not triumphs of an evolutionary process, nor is government "a reflection on human nature" (as the authors of *The Federalist* supposed). It is instead an instrument of class-gender-race oppression that social liberators are obliged to destroy.

In this malevolent confrontation, radicals are faced with a serious dilemma. Because democracies like America's are premised on conservative views of human nature, they embrace their opponents. Their frameworks institutionalize change and accommodate the unexpected. The right of reform is written into law as a necessary part of the democratic process, just as tolerance for difference is its central value. Not only does American democracy *not* suppress its opposition, American democracy provides a haven even for those who hate it. The democratic founders were conservatives who believed in the power of second thoughts.

It is this very principle of tolerance that queer revolutionaries and radicals most loathe and reject, and it is this rejection that defines them as radicals. For radicals, tolerance is itself repressive because it denies their most cherished illusion, that *they* are the authentic voice of humanity, and theirs is the universal human truth. When the people reject their radical solutions, in their view it is not really the people rejecting them. It is only their "false consciousness."

As a result, radicals do not want integration into a democratic system or equal participation in a democratic state. Nothing could be more self-defeating for them than to be counted one among many. For radicals, accepting the idea of a democratic norm is colluding in one's own oppression. It is to embrace the perspective of the oppressor. But the radical's loyalty is to the revolutionary vision.

To the queer radical, this vision embraces gender and sex as well. "Formally, the state is male, in that objectivity is its norm," explains the author of "Fear of a Queer Planet." In the radical future, there will be no such male norms. In the radical conception of human freedom, the revolutionary goal is a state of infinite possibility where norms no longer exist. At a tenth-anniversary conference of the National Council for Research on Women, its feminist president cited the term "unwed mother" as an example of "androcentric bias" because "it presupposes that the norm is to be a *wed* mother." Norms are instruments of the class, race, and gender enemy. "Hetero-normative," "androcentric," "Eurocentric" describe the objectivities and standards of the ruling caste. For the radical, the very idea of the normal community—the nonqueer—is a mark of oppression.

It is in this sense that the idea of "queer" (the revolt against the normal) can be seen as the core inspiration for all those experiments that produced this century's political nightmares. To the revolutionary, all that exists deserves to perish.

Normality, of course, can be either descriptive or prescriptive, or both. A "normal procedure" in public health practice is a procedure that is *usually* prescribed. It is usually prescribed because it has been previously tried and proven productive. It is by such trial and error that we arrive at the methods, procedures, institutions, laws, that bring our efforts into conformity with the orders of our nature.

When homosexuals object to the term "abnormal," they are object-
ing to its prescriptive use, for example the claim that homosexuality is
unnatural or immoral or should be illegal. As a matter of description,
however, homosexuality appears to be both a fact of nature and abnormal. According to the best statistics available, between 2 and 5 percent of
a population will be homosexual in any given society, whether that society is tolerant or intolerant of homosexual behavior. Studies of identical
twins indicate that upbringing has little bearing on homosexual development. The conservative conclusion will be that homosexuality is normal
in that it is rooted in nature, but that socially it is abnormal, in that the
vast majority of people are not and will never be homosexually inclined.

Description does not necessarily lead to prescriptive conclusions. The
fact that homosexuality is socially abnormal does not lead to any conclusion, for example, as to whether it is immoral or not. Such conclusions are
matters of private conviction or communal preference. Many communities and religions do view homosexuality as immoral. These attitudes may
be "oppressive" to homosexuals, but no more so than are some gentile attitudes toward Jews as souls condemned to eternal damnation. Jews may
not like these attitudes, but they can live with them in a society that pro-
tects their rights as citizens and invokes tolerance of difference as its central virtue: *e pluribus unum*. Homosexuals can as well. They do not need
to be "validated" by communities that disapprove of them. They need
only to be accepted as citizens who are equal before the law.

The demand that homosexuality be made illegal, on the other hand,
would not be merely a matter of communal preference. It would be a demand for exclusion that violates the American social contract and its pluralist imperative, running counter to the very idea of America's identity as
a nation. The ideal of American pluralism—the political norm that gov-
erns the behavior of its citizens—is the necessary embrace of diverse communities, even communities in fundamental conflict with each other.
The pluralistic norm of American democracy requires that the deviant
community and its abnormal citizen (black, homosexual, immigrant,
Jew) be equal before the law and enjoy the same inalienable rights as

everyone else. To violate *this* norm, to break the law of America's social contract, is to invite terrible consequences, as the bloodiest and most shameful pages of America's history attest.

But it is precisely this inclusion, the normal "civil rights" solution to the problem of minority status—integration into America's civic community—that radicals reject. In this rejection, homosexual activists follow the lead of their radical peers who are at war with America and its social contract, and who promote "solutions" that are separatist and destructive. By rejecting America's normative institutions, while radically inventing the social future, queer radicals have invited the very retributions that have historically attended the systematic violation of natural order. In the process, they have created their own social Frankenstein (even without achieving state power) in the contemporary epidemic of AIDS.

WHO BUT A sexual radical would have failed to realize in 1969, the year of "Gay Liberation," that promiscuous anal sex, conducted with strangers, was unsanitary and dangerous, and a threat to public health? Yet, gay liberation was defined by its theorists as just that: promiscuous anal sex, and sex with strangers. This was sex that was "transformative." Gay liberation was a challenge to the repressive "sex-negative" culture of "hetero-normativity," i.e., the heterosexual and monogamous norms of Judaeo-Christian culture.

In 1970, the Gay Liberation Front issued a manifesto proclaiming: "We are a revolutionary homosexual group of men and women formed with the realization that complete liberation of all people cannot come about unless existing social institutions are abolished. We reject society's attempt to impose sexual roles and definitions of our nature." In the radical view, existing sexual norms reflected nothing about collective biological experience, but were merely a social construction to preserve the privileges of dominant groups. To violate them was not to court moral and biological disaster but to break the chains of sexual oppression.

Like black radicals before them, gay activists rejected the idea of integration into a normally functioning civil order. Gay liberation was identified with a sexual agenda that did not seek civic tolerance, respect, and integration into the public order of bourgeois life. Instead, it was defined as a defiant promiscuity, the overthrow of bourgeois morals and sexual restraints and, consequently, of bourgeois standards of public hygiene. Public health procedures and laws were politically constructed instruments of a repressive sexual order. In rejecting the prevailing norms, radical activists recognized no natural or moral barriers to the realization of their liberationist agenda.

The effect of this radical self-conception and agenda was immediate and unmistakable. In the three years at the end of the Sixties, during the flowering of the sexual revolution, the incidence of amoebiasis (a parasitic sexually transmitted disease) increased *fifty* times in San Francisco because of promiscuous oral-anal sex among gays, a practice known as "rimming." A Toronto leftist paper defended this practice, despite the known health consequences, in an article titled "Rimming as a Revolutionary Act."[6] During the next decade, in the face of multiple venereal contagions stemming directly from the rebellion itself, America's tolerant civil order responded not by repression of sexual deviance, but by making room for the sexual radicals and their revolutionary ideas. Liberal politicians loosened the legal restraints on sexual encounters between consenting adults and public officials proceeded to license sexual gymnasia called "bathhouses," where hundreds of gay males per establishment could nightly indulge in sexual free-for-alls with as many partners as possible. Public health officials also turned a blind eye toward the orgiastic activity in bookstore backrooms, bars and "glory hole" establishments that gay radicals had dedicated to anonymous public sex.

"One effect of gay liberation," a prominent gay doctor noted, "is that sex has been institutionalized and franchised. Twenty years ago, there may have been a thousand men on any one night having sex in New York baths or parks. Now there are ten or twenty thousand—at the baths, the back-room bars, bookstores, porno theaters, . . . and a wide range of other places as well."[7] By decade's end, a $100 million public sex industry was flourishing in the gay districts of urban centers across the nation, attended regularly by over 60 percent of their gay populations. These establishments were viewed by gay activists not as threats to community morals and health, but as homosexual "liberated zones." At the same time, natural forces began to assert themselves and with ever more devastating results.

A parallel explosion of sexually transmitted diseases had followed on the heels of the Sixties' sexual revolution among heterosexuals. Between 1960 and 1970, cases of gonorrhea in the United States doubled for *all* Americans (and would triple by 1980). There was a difference in degree, and therefore in kind, however, between the gay sexual revolution and its heterosexual counterpart. As a society without women, the gay male community lacked the restraint normally imposed by the less sexually promiscuous gender on heterosexual encounters.[8] In 1978, a survey of gay men revealed that only 14 percent were in a monogamous relationship, while 43 percent had 500 lifetime sex partners and fully one-third had had 1,000.[9] As a result of the "revolutionary" sexual practices prevailing in liberated gay communities, the increase in sexual infections was predictably—and astronomically—greater among gays than among "sex negative" heterosexuals. By the early Eighties, when AIDS was first identified, the prevalence of syphilis and gonorrhea among gay men was *several hundred times* that among comparable groups of heterosexuals.[10]

As opportunistic but still treatable infections flourished in the *petri* dish of the liberated culture, gay radicals escalated their defiance and rebellion. The tolerance and even cooperation of public health officials, and easy availability of penicillin and other antibiotics, reinforced their confidence in the midst of the epidemics that ravaged the vanguard. Overloaded venereal disease clinics actually became trysting places in the liberated culture. In his authoritative history of the epidemic, Randy Shilts described the upbeat atmosphere on the eve of the outbreak: "Gay men were being washed by tide after tide of increasingly serious infections. First it was syphilis and gonorrhea. Gay men made up about 80% of the 70,000 annual patient visits to [San Francisco's] VD clinics. Easy treatment had imbued them with such a cavalier attitude toward venereal diseases that many gay men saved their waiting-line numbers, like little tokens of desirability, and the clinic was considered an easy place to pick up both a shot and a date."[11]

Far from causing radical activists to rethink their agenda, the burgeoning sexual epidemics in their liberated zones prompted them to escalate the assault. When Dr. Dan William, a gay specialist, publicly warned of the danger of continued promiscuity, he was denounced as a "monogamist" in the gay press. When playwright Larry Kramer sounded a similar alarm, he was accused in the *New York Native* of "gay homophobia and anti-eroticism." At a public meeting in the year preceding the first AIDS cases, Edmund White, coauthor of *The Joy of Gay Sex,* proposed that "gay men should wear their sexually transmitted diseases like red badges of courage in a war against a sex-negative society." Michael Callen was a gay youth present at the meeting who was shortly to come down with AIDS. When he heard White's triumphant defiance of nature's law, he remembered thinking: "Every time I get the clap I'm striking a blow for the sexual revolution."[12]

In his book *Surviving AIDS,* Callen (who died of the disease in 1996) recounted his medical history:

> I calculated that since becoming sexually active in 1973, I had racked up more than three thousand different sex partners in bathhouses, back rooms, meat racks, and tearooms. As a consequence, I had also had the following sexually transmitted diseases, many more than once: hepatitis A, hepatitis B, hepatitis non-A/non-B; herpes simplex types I and II; venereal warts; amoebiasis and salmonella; syphilis; gonorrhea; nonspecific arthritis; chlamydia; cytomegalovirus and Epstein-Barr virus mononucleosis; and eventually cryptosporidiosis.

Callen's experience was emblematic. The first clusters of AIDS victims were formed not by monogamous civil reformers who had come out of the closet to demand tolerance and respect, but by sexual revolutionaries who rejected in its totality the existing system of morality and social constraint, who disregarded their own experience and pushed their bodies' immune envelopes in order to seize pleasure and advance the new order. "One strain of seventies gay liberationist rhetoric proclaimed that sex was inherently liberating, . . ." writes Callen. "In other words, I should consider myself more liberated if I'd had a thousand sex partners than if I'd only had five hundred. Some of us believed we could change the world through sexual liberation and that we were taking part in a noble experiment."[13] After being stricken himself, Callen reflected on the revolutionary path he had pursued: "Unfortunately, as a function of a microbiological . . . certainty, this level of sexual activity resulted in concurrent epidemics of syphilis, gonorrhea, hepatitis, amoebiasis, venereal warts and, we discovered too late, other pathogens. Unwittingly, and with the best of revolutionary intentions, a small subset of gay men managed to create disease settings equivalent to those of poor Third World nations in one of the richest nations on earth."[14]

The diseases were being transformed as well. As Shilts explains, the enteric diseases—amoebiasis, gay bowel syndrome, giardiasis and shigellosis—were followed by an epidemic of hepatitis B, "a disease that had transformed itself, via the popularity of anal intercourse, from a blood-borne scourge into a venereal disease."[15] By 1981, 73 percent of the gay males in San Francisco were found to be infected by hepatitis B, a disease that not only kills in some cases, but permanently lowers the immune systems of the hosts it has invaded.[16]

Where were public health officials, who certainly knew and understood these facts, as the epidemics tallied their victims? Why didn't these officials intervene, sound the alarm, close the bathhouses, undertake vigorous education campaigns among gays to warn potential victims of the danger in their path? The reason was the revolution itself. When confronted by these questions, Don Francis of the Centers for Disease Control, a leading figure in the battle against AIDS, admitted: "We didn't intervene because we felt that it would be interfering with an alternative lifestyle."[17] So successful was the defense of "gay culture" by radical activists that it made traditional public health practices politically impossible. When officials did attempt to close the sexual bathhouses, the epidemic's breeding grounds, they were passionately attacked by gay political leaders who defended public sex establishments as "symbols of gay liberation." In the words of sex radical Michael Warner,

> The phenomenology of a sex club encounter is an experience of world making. It's an experience of being connected not just to this person, but to potentially limitless numbers of people, and that's why it's important that it be with a stranger.[18]

To close the sex establishments, as a matter of public health policy, would pose a threat to liberation, to the idea of a queer identity and the project of overthrowing sex-negative and sex-specific norms.

The surrender of CDC officials like Francis to these political imperatives was a testament to the influence the increasingly powerful gay lobby was now able to exert. Explaining why public health officials did not address the reckless practices of the bathhouse culture, gay journalist Gabriel Rotello, observed: "[Public health officials] feared that by focusing on the diseases spawned by the gay sexual revolution they would be accused of homophobia. Gay leaders frequently made it plain to researchers that anyone who raised questions about gay sexual freedom for any reason, whether ethical or biological, would be equally accused of anti-gay bias. Few researchers were willing to venture into such a political and social hot zone, and the few who did found that they consequently lost influence within the gay male community, a bad position to be in if your research required a high level of cooperation from gay men."[19]

These political attitudes led to tragic consequences. In 1983, Dr. Joseph Sonnabend had observed that the disease was occurring in a "subset" of gay men "characterized by having had sexual contact with large numbers of different partners in settings where the carriage of . . . sexually transmitted infections is high." Later epidemiological studies confirmed that the existence of "core groups" of men engaging in high levels of sexual activity with concurrent multiple partners was the crucial factor in creating and sustaining the AIDS epidemic. As a blood-borne virus, principally passed through torn or damaged membranes, the infection was very difficult to transmit. An HIV carrier was only contagious during two periods in the course of the infection. To engage in *anal* sex with *multiple* partners in these windows was thus crucial for crossing the epidemic threshold. The bathhouses and sex establishments, which facilitated anal sex with multiple, concurrent and anonymous partners, were ideally (and in many ways uniquely) suited for this grim accomplishment.

Drawing the connection between the political culture of gay liberation in the 1970s and the epidemic metastasizing in its midst, Rotello analyzed the deadly equation of social revolution and disease:

> Multiple concurrent partners, versatile anal sex, core group behavior centered in commercial sex establishments, widespread recreational drug abuse, repeated waves of STDs and constant intake of antibiotics, sexual tourism and travel—these factors were not "accidents." Multi-partner anal sex was encouraged, celebrated, considered a central component of liberation. Core group behavior in baths and sex clubs was deemed by many the quintessence of freedom. Versatility was declared a political imperative. Analingus was pronounced the champagne of gay sex, a palpable gesture of revolution. STDs were to be worn like badges of honor, antibiotics to be taken with pride. Far from being accidents, these things characterized the very foundation of what it supposedly meant to experience gay liberation. Taken together they formed a sexual ecology of almost incalculably catastrophic dimensions, a classic feedback loop in which virtually every factor served to amplify every other. From the virus's point of view, the ecology of liberation was a royal road to adaptive triumph. From many gay men's point of view, it proved a trapdoor to hell on earth.[20]

In an article that appeared in 1997 in the gay magazine *The Advocate*, Larry Kramer, author of *The Normal Heart* and founder of the Gay Men's Health Crisis summed up this equation in an epigraph: "We have made sex the cornerstone of gay liberation and gay culture, and it has killed us."[21]

The crucial role of politics not only in creating but in sustaining the spread of the infection was evident from its early progress. In the early Eighties, the epidemic was still confined to three cities with large homosexual communities—New York, San Francisco and Los Angeles. In this early stage, aggressive public health methods might have prevented the contagion's outward spread, particularly into the Hispanic and black populations that became the loci of its next explosions. But every effort to take the precautionary measures normal in the treatment of epidemics was thwarted by the political juggernaut the gay liberation movement had created. Under pressure from gay activists, the public health directors in the principal affected communities resisted the closing of bathhouses, maintaining that such closures would be an assault on the gains that gay liberation had achieved, that they would violate the gay community's "civil rights," and that, in any case, the bathhouses were valuable centers of "education" about AIDS, even though their only purpose was to facilitate anonymous promiscuous sex. In fact, it was because promiscuous sex was central to the idea of gay liberation that the institutions that made these activities possible had to be defended. As a result, even though some bathhouses in San Francisco and other locales were eventually closed in the mid-Eighties, they were soon reopened.

Other prevention policies, like contact tracing and testing, were also met with political opposition on the grounds that such measures were "transformative"—in other words, that they entailed behavioral and political changes that would put the revolution at risk. During the herpes epidemic of the Seventies, public health authorities had closed sex clubs in heterosexual communities and put them out of business. But in the gay community, even after the advent of AIDS and despite its greater gravity as a public health concern, revolutionary politics demanded that gay sex clubs be kept open. Closing bathhouses, gay leaders warned, would drive the carriers of AIDS and their potential victims "underground," where public health officials and programs could not reach them. The same argument was used to reject mandatory testing of high-risk groups and contact tracing of infected parties to contain the epidemic's spread.[22] Such measures, it was said, would drive those at risk away from public health services.

As late as 1995, with 900,000 individuals infected, the board of the New York Gay Men's Health Crisis still opposed closing bathhouses and sex clubs with arguments that "wholesale closure would not cause unsafe sex to disappear but would disperse such activity to parks, alleys, underground clubs and other covert locales where participants would be subject to arrest or violence, and where HIV prevention interventions could not easily reach." By then, studies had already shown, however, that the brief closing of some bathhouses in the mid-Eighties had caused a dramatic drop in unsafe sex practices.[23]

In addition to being unfounded, the warning that bathhouse closures and testing procedures would drive the problem underground was also an implicit threat: If government officials attempted to pursue traditional public health policies, they would lose the cooperation of the political leadership of the gay community. Instead of being seen as helpers, public officials would be cast in their historic role as persecutors. Pre-Stonewall memories of vice-squad arrests would be revived. Official testing of the gay community would be portrayed as the first step in a campaign to restigmatize gays as second-class citizens, perhaps even to round them up for incarceration.

Faced with the hostility of gay leaders and the prospect of a gay community gripped by paranoia and refusing its cooperation, public health officials decided to take the path of least resistance. Suppressing what they knew to be medically sound and morally required, they shelved the traditional public health defenses that had been used successfully against epidemics in the past. As Ronald Bayer, a professor at the Columbia University School of Public Health, wrote in a book published ten years after the onset of the epidemic: "U.S. officials had no alternative but to negotiate the course of AIDS policy with representatives of a well-organized gay community and their allies in the medical and political establishments. In this process, many of the traditional practices of public health that might have been brought to bear were dismissed as inappropriate."[24]

Not only did the political power of the gay liberationists thwart measures available to prevent the spread of the epidemic from its three geographical areas of origin, they obstructed measures that would have prevented it from spilling over into other communities. Thus, when officials tried to institute screening procedures for the nation's blood banks and asked homosexuals not to donate while the epidemic persisted, gay political leaders denounced the moratorium and opposed the procedures as efforts that would infringe the "right" of gays to give blood. The San Francisco Coordinating Committee of Gay and Lesbian Services, chaired by Pat Norman—a city official who was lesbian and black, but without a medical background—issued a policy paper asserting that donor screening was "reminiscent of miscegenation blood laws that divided black blood from white" and "similar in concept to the World War II rounding up of Japanese-Americans in the western half of the country to minimize the possibility of espionage."[25] The result of these attitudes was to spread AIDS among hemophiliacs and drug-using heterosexuals, and among black and Hispanic populations that soon accounted for more than 50 percent of the infected.

The same attitudes had made it possible for the small subset of gays involved in core group sexual activity to bridge the epidemic into the gay population at large. Traditionally, social stigmas create a wall between members of a population who rebel against norms and engage in destructive behaviors. The poor, the diseased, the rootless, the socially marginal, are normally shunned by the majority. But by its very nature, as a movement to overthrow the normal, the gay revolution had removed these protective barriers. The removal of stigmas and the inversion of values was an essential part of the project to liberate gays from heteronormativity, sex negativity and the oppression of an ordered world. Even as the disease spread and took its terrible human toll, no prejudice or stigma attached to those who engaged in bathhouse orgies. They were "beautiful, well-heeled men who were both the most sexually active and the most desirable. . . . Indeed, many people felt the behavior of [these] gay men represented the apex of gay liberation, something to be envied and emulated rather than shunned."[26]

As a result of the political campaigns launched by gay activists, it has not been possible for public health officials to gather the most basic information required to fight an epidemic, namely, who is infected with the virus and which communities are at risk. The primary method available to public health workers to combat epidemic infections is to identify both the carriers and groups at risk and then try to separate them, whether by quarantine or education.[27] Identifying carrier groups requires testing when the symptoms of the disease do not appear immediately, as in the case of AIDS, which can have a latency of ten years. Yet, in 1985, when the government was ready to announce the licensing of the first test for detecting the presence of the HIV virus, the National Gay Task Force and the Lambda Legal Defense and Education Fund (a gay civil rights group) petitioned the federal courts to delay the licensing of the test, pending a legal guarantee that it would *not* be used for widespread screening of gay men.[28] The government acceded to the radicals' wishes. At the same time, and for the same reason, the CDC decided not to include HIV infection as a reportable disease.

As a result of political pressures exerted by gay activists and their allies in organizations like the ACLU and the Democratic Party, there has been no general testing of the population at risk in the two decades since the onset of the epidemic. Nor has there been any systematic contact tracing, which is standard for combating sexually transmitted diseases. Nor has there been any systematic reporting of the incidence of infection. Only after the full-blown disease has struck its victim do public health officials take notice. As Chandler Burr observed in an article in the *Atlantic Monthly* written nearly twenty years after the first AIDS fatalities:

> Although the disease called AIDS must be reported by name in all fifty states, infection with HIV, the virus that causes AIDS, need not be: only twenty-six states mandate the (confidential) reporting by name of positive test results for HIV, and these states tend to be ones with modest caseloads. Twelve states—including California and New York, by far the two worst-afflicted states—have no broad reporting requirements for HIV.[29]

To avoid reporting HIV infection, most states do not even classify HIV as a "sexually transmitted disease." As of 1995, in fact, only twelve states had so classified AIDS and HIV. Thus, although the federal government spends over $4 billion annually to fight AIDS, no government agency really knows how many people are HIV-positive, nor where the disease is spreading. While the Centers for Disease Control estimate that the number of Americans infected with HIV is as high as 900,000, only half are thought to be aware of their infection.

Lee Reichman, executive director of the New Jersey Medical School National Tuberculosis Center, summarized this situation in an interview with Chandler Burr: "Traditional public health is absolutely effective at controlling infectious disease. It should have been applied to AIDS from the start, and it wasn't. Long before there was AIDS, there were other sexually transmitted diseases, and you had partner notification and testing and reporting. This was routine public health at its finest, and this is the way sexually transmitted diseases were controlled."[30] A prominent epidemiologist, also quoted by Burr, discreetly concurred: "We have convinced ourselves that the fight for survival can be waged in a way that is socially acceptable but not always biologically credible."[31]

Throughout the epidemic, the only measures of AIDS prevention socially acceptable to gay revolutionaries were those which passed the political test that the measures adopted be the least "transformative," that they present the least challenge to the revolution itself. Rather than closing the bathhouses and sex clubs, rather than testing, rather than contact tracing and reporting, the liberationists insisted that the government focus on AIDS research and AIDS education. Almost all other measures and actions were successfully opposed as threats to the civil rights of homosexuals and to the gains of gay liberation—in other words, as aggressions against the liberated zone.

Even the politically acceptable policy of "AIDS education," however, was subjected by gay leaders to ideological scrutiny. As a result, the education campaign was given two crucial political spins that crippled its usefulness as a weapon against the epidemic. The first was to emphasize the "nondiscriminatory" aspect of AIDS; the second was to obscure the principal sexual path of AIDS transmission.

At the time the education campaign was launched, the AIDS epidemic was still virtually confined to the homosexual community. In San Francisco, in 1983, over 95 percent of the infections were of gay males.

(In New York, where intravenous drug use was prevalent, the overall figure was lower, but among cases involving *sexual* transmission, again over 95 percent of those infected were gay males.) The AIDS epidemic had not spread to the heterosexual community for good reasons. Vaginal intercourse was a poor transmission channel for the virus, and the relatively low promiscuity rates for heterosexuals also made the rapid spread of the virus problematic. Equally important was the absence of a political apparatus dedicated to the idea of sexual liberation (an absence that allowed the closing of heterosexual sex clubs).

Despite these realities, the gay community insisted on and got a federally funded AIDS "education" campaign that did not single out anal sex as the primary path of transmission and that was not specifically directed to the at-risk homosexual community. Despite the concentration of sexually transmitted AIDS among homosexuals, the government education campaign also targeted the vastly larger but not at-risk population of heterosexuals. An expensive, aggressive and wasteful effort was mounted to persuade heterosexuals that "AIDS Is An Equal-Opportunity Virus" and about to explode in their own communities. This "de-gaying of AIDS" was thought to have the political advantage of gaining more sympathy for the affected communities and thus more money for AIDS programs. But it also diluted the amount of dollars specifically available for the communities at risk. One government pamphlet issued by Surgeon General Everett Koop was sent to 107 million Americans warning them that "AIDS doesn't discriminate" and that the epidemic was a threat to all.[32] In 1987, Koop declared that AIDS cases overall are "going to increase ninefold . . . between now and 1990. But among heterosexuals there are going to be twenty times as many cases, so that perhaps 10 percent of the patients will be heterosexual."[33] In fact, throughout the epidemic, no more than 4 percent of the cases were the result of heterosexual transmission.

Even more significant than the attempt to scare heterosexuals into regarding themselves as an at-risk group was the success of gay political activists in preventing the words "promiscuous anal sex" from appearing in education literature along with any mention of the primary role played by bathhouses and sex clubs in the spread of the epidemic. Under political pressure, the official AIDS "education" campaign failed to warn even those potential victims it did reach about the specific danger they faced.

This deference to political correctness affected more than government propaganda. It also controlled the information provided on the editorial pages and in the news features of the nation's press. Until a *Wall Street Journal* article broke the general press silence in 1996, not a single major newspaper, or radio or television news service, had challenged the myth of a heterosexual epidemic, or questioned the wisdom of propagating such a myth even though the statistics published regularly by the CDC itself showed that no such epidemic existed.[34] On the contrary, the press actively promoted the false impression of a general epidemic, as in a famous *Newsweek* cover which showed ordinary Americans of no particular sexual orientation as the typical carriers of AIDS.[35] As part of its ongoing support for the politically correct view of the epidemic demanded by gay pressure groups, the press refused to investigate the role of the bathhouses, or to explore the issues of testing, contact tracing and public health reporting, even as the infection raged and hundreds of thousands died.

Gabriel Rotello sums up the consequences of the politicization of AIDS within the gay community in these terms: "The enterprise of AIDS prevention in the gay world has never included a sober evaluation of the ways the sexual culture of the Seventies produced the AIDS epidemic. Quite the opposite. The enterprise of AIDS prevention in the gay world has strenuously avoided any detailed examination of these mechanisms. Their very discussion is considered offensive, homophobic, self-loathing. Instead, we have sought to minimize or even deny these factors, partly in order to preserve as much as possible the gains of the gay sexual revolution—the very 'gains' that brought us AIDS."[36]

The establishment of a party line, and the obstruction of politically incorrect reporting of AIDS issues, not only paralyzed the gay community and blocked effective prevention efforts but, because of the power of the political Left and its liberal allies, controlled the nation's public health policy as well. From the beginning, national AIDS policy has observed the strict parameters established by the "progressive" attitude toward the epidemic. It has focused exclusively on politically approved education programs and the pursuit of medical antidotes—the "magic bullets" of a vaccine and a cure, which would allow the sexual revolution to proceed without impediment.

Like the misdirected education programs, the emphasis on medical research has also been, in part, a costly detour from the development of an effective public health defense. At the very outset of the epidemic, the medical consensus was already far from optimistic about the possibility of such a medical fix. Because of the nature of the HIV retrovirus, it was generally agreed that there would not be a vaccine for ten years and maybe never a cure.[37] More than ten years later, the quest for a vaccine is still in the future, and there is still no AIDS cure. Meanwhile, more money has been spent on AIDS research per patient death than on any disease in history. On an annual basis, for example, the AIDS money government provides is *ten times* per patient death the amount allocated for combating breast and ovarian cancer, to say nothing of prostate cancer, which kills more men annually than AIDS.

Even more significant than the draining of resources has been the role that the hope of a cure has played in deflecting energy and attention from the strategy of prevention. Only one preventive measure acceptable to the liberationist perspective possessed the potential to interrupt the epidemic. This was the use of condoms in the practice of "safe sex." The campaign to advocate the use of prophylactics was judged not to have counterrevolutionary implications because promiscuous activity—even promiscuous activity with strangers in "core group" settings—could be continued without stigma under the principle of "safe sex." An additional political advantage lay in the fact that both gays and heterosexuals would be able to use condoms and both would be targets of any government propaganda effort, thus avoiding the stigma of responsibility to the community actually at risk.

By the end of the epidemic's second decade, however, it was evident that the safe sex campaign had not worked. Condoms were not 100 percent reliable, and surveys showed that more than half the gay community did not use them consistently. As a result, the safe sex effort failed to slow the seroconversion rate to levels below the critical epidemic threshold. In 1991, a report published in the *American Journal of Epidemiology* reported a "second wave" of the epidemic, concluding that the overall probability of a twenty-year-old gay man contracting HIV was still 20 percent by age twenty-five and about 50 percent by age fifty-five.[38] After more than a decade of AIDS education, safe sex and other "nontransformative" campaigns, and despite the deaths of several hundred thousand gay males, the rates of infection were still high enough to infect half the gay population and sustain a major epidemic.

At the core of the problem in combating the epidemic remained the "institutions of gay liberation" still protected by the political efforts of gay activists and their liberal allies in government. After a brief closure in some locales, the bathhouses and commercial sex clubs were operating again as engines of infection, providing settings where high levels of multipartner sexual activity could take place. "By 1995," Gabriel Rotello reported, "one could witness all forms of unprotected sex almost any night of the week in many of [New York's] most popular sex clubs catering to gay men."[39]

By 1995, Rotello and several other prominent gay activists, including Larry Kramer, the founder of ACT UP, and Michelangelo Signorile, a founder of Queer Nation, had had second thoughts about the liberated zones that their movement had created, and which they now realized were the crucial breeding grounds of the epidemic. Determined to rectify their earlier mistake, they formed an organization called Gay and Lesbian HIV Prevention Activists (GALPHA) and were even prepared to appeal directly to public health authorities to monitor and if necessary close the public sources of infection, as they should have done at the beginning of the epidemic.[40]

But, as in the epidemic's early years, this attempt to close the sex clubs was opposed by gay activists on the grounds that such closures were "homophobic" and would undo the gains of gay liberation. A group of activists, including the author of "Fear of a Queer Planet" formed a counterorganization called Sex Panic to oppose such measures. They argued that individuals possessed a "right to unsafe sex," and repeated the claim that the sex clubs were institutions of gay liberation.[41]

In the golden age of that liberation, the author and "sexual outlaw" John Rechy had explained that promiscuity was gay men's way of "taking the revolution to the streets." Activist Michael Bronski reiterated the theme twenty-five years later in the gay magazine *Steam*: "Gay liberation means sexual freedom. And sexual freedom means more sex, better sex, sex in the bushes, in the toilets, in the baths, sex without love, sex without harassment, sex at home and sex in the streets." Reflecting the radical view, Bronski complained that the AIDS crisis had given rise to "solipsistic, homophobic theories . . . about why *less* sex is good" and urged the community to reject such ideas. In a 1997 symposium on the conflict over closing the bathhouses, the gay bishop of Los Angeles's Unity Fellowship Church expressed the passion still invested in the idea of gay liberation: "I might teach and share spirituality, and bring holiness into the lives of my [gay] parishoners, but at the same time I would die for their right to have a sex club."[42] Gay theorist Douglas Crimp, a member of Sex Panic, summarized the revolutionaries' response to the "second wave": "They insist that our promiscuity will destroy us, when in fact it is our promiscuity that will save us."[43]

The source of this gay bravado lay in the recurrent and misplaced faith that science would one day provide a "magic bullet" in the form of a vaccine or an antiviral antidote, allowing the revolution to proceed without obstruction by natural forces. Advances had indeed been made in the development of antiviral "cocktails" that reduced the AIDS death rate, albeit falling far short of a cure. But the response to this development had been reduced fear of the infection, the revival of the sex club culture, and the launching of the "Circuit," an international series of weekend-long sex parties attended by tens of thousands of young gays.

To epidemiologists, there was no surprise in these developments. The precedents of other epidemics showed that even a true "cure," though saving many lives, would not spell the end of the epidemic itself, in the absence of morally enforced social norms, and could even intensify it. Gonorrhea and syphilis were epidemic until the mid-forties, when the newly discovered drug penicillin offered the prospect of a 100 percent cure. Many predicted these drugs would wipe out the diseases for good, and for two decades the infection rates of both did dramatically drop. But changing moral norms and the prospect of casual sex without fear of life-threatening illness caused people to become less cautious in their sexual practices and eventually revived both viruses. Between 1965 and 1975, during the heyday of the radical "counterculture," the incidence of gonorrhea tripled, while syphilis quadrupled, making the latter the most common infectious disease in the nation.[44] The repeated use of newer and more powerful antibiotics to control these diseases, moreover, produced strains that are now drug-resistant. The lesson is clear: in the absence of behavioral changes and the restoration of traditional sexual norms, the prospect of new epidemics from AIDS-related viruses will continue and may even increase.

The war against civilization and nature, which is at the heart of the radical enterprise, inevitably produces monsters like AIDS. The epidemic has now killed 300,000 Americans, with three times as many infected. But who knows how many have actually been stricken, since even at this late date there is still no systematic testing or scientific reporting, while the implementation of real public health methods is nowhere in sight. Thus, even as the ashes of the Communist empire grow cold, the moral and political lessons of its disasters have not been learned. The nihilism that rejects nature and the idea of the normal as it sets out to create a radical new world, though predictable in its consequences, is as blindly destructive as ever. Once in power, as the entire history of our bloody century attests, the radical impulse embraces radical evil in the never ending attempt to enforce its mandate and realize its impossible ideal.

CHAPTER SIX

A CONSERVATIVE
HOPE

A LITTLE MORE THAN A YEAR AFTER THE COLLAPSE OF Communism, the Heritage Foundation organized a series of lectures on conservative ideas. One of the topics was "Are We Conservatives?" a fact that already tells us something about the subject itself. One could no more imagine posing the question "Are we progressives?" to a comparable gathering of the Left than one could ask a group of citizens "Are We Americans?" without risking insult and rancorous debate. To raise such issues in such contexts would be to question an identity and the foundations of a faith.

The very ability to ask the question "Are We Conservatives?" therefore, tells us that conservatism is not an ideology in the sense that liberalism, or the various forms of radicalism are. Conservatism is not an "identity politics," addressed before all else to the issue of what kind of people embrace it. It is not a politics whose primary concern is to place its adherents in the camp of moral humanity and thus to confer on them the stamp of History's approval. Because conservatism is not a philosophy that seeks to enlist its adherents in a historical vanguard, it does not have a "party line." It is possible for conservatives to question most positions held by other conservatives, including, evidently, the notion that they are conservatives at all, without risking ex-communication, expulsion from the community, or even a raised eyebrow. Of course, this latitude has limits. No one would regard as conservative someone who embraced the leveling aspirations of contemporary liberalism or the utopian agendas of the socialist Left. Within such limits, however, the liberality of conservatism (or at least American conservatism) is a generally underappreciated fact.

Although not an ideological faith, American conservatism *is* grounded in philosophical convictions, which makes it unique. Conservatism is traditionally a disposition rather than a coherent philosophical doctrine. Even as a philosophic stance, however, American conservatism evolves from considerations that are ultimately pragmatic. To say this is not to deny that conservatives often claim religious principles as the basis for their convictions. But it is not a religious commitment that distinguishes them as conservatives. There are radicals and liberals who have religious commitments and make similar claims.

To say that conservative attitudes derive from pragmatic considerations is to state an obvious but important fact: what makes conservative principles "conservative" is that they are rooted in an attitude about the *past* rather than in expectations of the future. It is this pragmatic foundation that explains why conservatism can be the common ground of such diverse viewpoints. Conservatives operate from what are often profoundly different philosophical assumptions, and entertain quite divergent expectations about the social future and what it might be.

Indeterminacy about the future does not mean that conservatives are indifferent to social outcomes. They would like to see social arrangements that are relatively more benevolent and measurably more humane. But they are only able to endorse specific institutions as prudential guides through passages that are uncertain and despite consequences that may be unintended. Unlike radicals, conservatives do not pretend to be able to shape the social future by bending it to their will. They do not offer plans designed to remake human beings by inducing them to act in ways that are dramatically different from how human beings have acted in the past.

The "first principles" of conservatism, then, are propositions about the existing social contract, about the nature of human beings in a social context, as established by historical experience. They are propositions about limits, and what limits make possible. It is this attention to practical experience and emphasis on workable arrangements that explains why conservatives can be liberal and tolerant toward their opponents in ways that progressives cannot.

In contrast to conservatism, liberal and radical ideologies are about desired, and therefore determinate, futures. The first principles of the Left are the principles of constructing a "better world." The radical future is to be consciously designed by enlightened intelligence. It is a basic characteristic of the progressive outlook that it proposes a sharp break with the experience of the past, and that its visions entail a rejection of existing social contracts.

Throughout the modern era, progressives have proposed a future in which all of society's members are to be made equal in their economic and social conditions—or, at the very least, in their starting points. This is the future that radicals call "socially just." Those who share the progressive outlook may differ about the degree of equality that might be achieved in the name of social justice, or the means acceptable for arriving at such a state. (The concession liberals make when they refer to "leveling the playing field," as opposed to leveling the players, results from their recognition of previous failures.) But the differences between liberals and radicals are confined to degrees in the results desired, and in the means by which these results may be obtained. The goal of achieving "social justice" and of using the state to enforce desired outcomes remains the same. It is this shared utopianism that makes it appropriate to refer to both liberalism and radicalism as ideologies of the Left.

Since ideologies of the Left derive from commitments to an imagined future, to question them is to provoke a moral rather than an empirical response: *Are you for or against the equality of human beings?* To demur from a commitment to the progressive viewpoint is thus not a failure to agree on relevant facts but an unwillingness to embrace the liberated future. Worse, it is to *will* the imperfections of the unliberated present. In the current political cant of the Left, it is to be racist, sexist, and classist—a defender of the oppressive status quo.

That is why not only radicals, but even those who call themselves liberals, are instinctively intolerant toward their conservative opponents. For progressives, the future is not a maze of human uncertainty and unintended consequence. It is a moral choice. To achieve the socially just future requires only that enough people decide to bring it into being. Consequently, it is perfectly consistent for progressives to consider themselves morally tolerant and intellectually enlightened while demonizing their opponents as immoral, ignorant and radically evil.

While the politics of the Left is derived from assumptions about the liberated future, its partisans are also careful to construct a view of history that validates the claim. At the outset of the Cold War, the sociologist T. H. Marshall delivered a famous lecture on the "development of citizenship" in the West. In it, he distinguished between the civil, political and social dimensions of citizenship, identifying each of the last three centuries as a stage in their progress. The revolutions of the Eighteenth Century institutionalized *civil* rights of free speech and religion, and a government of laws. The Nineteenth Century extended the rights of suffrage and the *political* base of freedom, establishing the equality of individuals as participants in the political process that guaranteed their civil rights. The Twentieth Century—then at its midpoint—was witnessing a revolution that would extend citizenship rights to the social and economic realms, by recognizing entitlements to education, health care, material well-being, and security, as basic human rights.[1]

It should be obvious that this third sphere of citizenship rights embraces the prescriptions of socialism, and that Marshall's paradigm of human progress is merely a liberal formulation of the agenda of the modern Left. For two centuries, the Left has attempted to "complete" the French Revolution by extending political and civil freedom into the social realm in the form of redistributionist claims to economic wealth. "Socialism" is the programmatic template for this project, and its historic failure refutes once and for all the idea of progress that Marshall embraced.

Modern conservatism begins with the recognition that the progressive agenda and its progressive paradigm are bankrupt. They have been definitively refuted by the catastrophes of socialism in the Twentieth Century. The utopian quest for social justice and its redistributionist goals are implicated in those catastrophes as root causes of the totalitarian fate. To propose a "solution" that is utopian—in plain English, impossible—is to propose a solution that requires absolute coercion. Who wills the end wills the means.

Post-Communist conservatism, then, begins with the principle that is written in the blood of these social experiments. It was summed up by Friedrich Hayek in *The Constitution of Liberty* more than thirty years ago: "It is just not true," he wrote, "that human beings are born equal; . . . if we treat them equally, the result must be inequality in their actual position; . . . [thus] the only way to place them in an equal position would be to treat them differently. Equality before the law and material equality are, therefore, not only different but in conflict with each other."

In other words, the rights historically claimed in the paradigm of the Left are self-contradicting and self-defeating. The history of the social experiments of the last two hundred years describes the stark implications of that contradiction and the terrible price of those defeats. The regime of social justice, of which the Left dreams, is a regime that by its very nature must crush individual freedom. It is not a question of choosing the right (while avoiding the wrong) political means in order to achieve the desired ends. The means are contained in the ends. The leftist revolution must crush freedom *in order* to achieve the "social justice" that it seeks. It is unable, therefore, to achieve even that end. This is the totalitarian circle that cannot be squared. Socialism is not bread without freedom; it is neither freedom nor bread. The shades of the victims in the endless cemetery of Twentieth-Century revolutions cry out from their still fresh graves: *the liberated future is a destructive illusion.* To heed this cry is the beginning of a conservative point of view.

That point of view is most succinctly summarized in Hayek's observation that "the prevailing belief in 'social justice' is at present probably
the gravest threat to most other values of a free civilization."[2] The reason
is that the idea of social justice is a chimera and that it incorporates the
totalitarian idea. In order for the term "social justice" to have meaning, as
Hayek pointed out, there must be an entity "society" that can be held responsible for perceived injustices, such as the unequal distribution of
wealth. But there is no such entity. The unequal distribution of wealth
flows from the free choices of individuals in the economic market. The
only practical meaning that complaints about social injustice have, therefore, is that a system exists in which individuals are free to choose their
occupations, to succeed and to fail, and there is no power to make the results "correspond to our wishes."[3] In other words, the only remedy for
"social injustice" is for a state to abrogate individual freedoms, eliminate
such choices, and organize the social order to correspond to *its* conception of what is morally right. The demand for "social justice," consistently advanced, is really the demand for a command economy organized
by a totalitarian state.

Even when its designs are unrealized, however, the very quest for social justice inevitably leads to social division and group conflict, whether
of race, gender or class. Consider this characteristic assertion by the left-
wing critic Garry Wills: "By the standards of any other society, or of reason itself, the great and growing disparity of wealth in America is a form
of successful class warfare waged against the poor and the moderately
well-off." Ignore the empirical claim about disparate wealth (which is
false, but in any case irrelevant) and focus instead on the means by which
this disparity is alleged to have been accomplished—a "successful class
warfare." What possible meaning can these words have? Who has waged
this war against the poor? What agency has singled out these individuals
(rather than others) to hobble them in the scramble for economic re-
wards? How does Wills's view account for the liberal majorities that have
dominated American governments since the inception of the New Deal,
instituting progressive income taxes and welfare measures that have re-
distributed trillions of dollars in transfer payments from the wealthy to

the poor? If the wealthy are able to create the poor by ruthless "class warfare," why are they then not able to control the state and block its redistributionist programs? Wills's statement has, in fact, no empirical meaning. It is just the emotional gas of the Left. But the destructive implications of such incitements are undeniable.[4]

While opposing the destructive chimera of socialist justice, however, conservatives should refrain from indulging in a utopianism of their own. The conservative vision does not exclude compromise, nor should it condemn every attempt, however moderate, to square the circle of political liberty and human welfare. In particular, conservatism does not require that all aspects of the welfare state be rejected in favor of free-market principles. After all, conservatives are (or should be) the first to recognize the intractable nature of the human condition and the problems it creates. The perfectly free society is as untenable as the perfectly just one, and for the same reason. We would have to rip out our all-too-human hearts in order to achieve it. Some economic redistribution may be compassionate and necessary, even though (as Hayek has shown) it can never be just.

In short, within conservatism there is room for a "liberal" argument as to how far we need to go in following the logic of liberty and how widely we can extend the social safety net, or best shape the contours of a welfare-intending state. But for conservatives, it is the limits of such endeavors that need to be appreciated at the outset, the dangers of stepping beyond those limits that must be understood.

The Hayekian paradox—the point from which contemporary conservatism begins—is, of course, only a reformulation of an understanding shared by the architects of the American founding. Thus, the incompatibility of liberty with any plan to eliminate inequality and difference is the essential argument Madison makes in *The Federalist*, No. 10.[5] Nor is it an accident, as Marxists like to say, that Madison describes the constitutional arrangement as a design specifically to thwart the projects of the Left—"a rage for paper money, for an abolition of debts, for an equal division of property, or for any other improper or wicked project."

It is in the constitutional founding that American conservatism finds its true philosophical ground. American conservatives define themselves first of all as conservers of the constitutional framework. The philosophy of that framework informs their outlook. This philosophy originates in a conservative appreciation of limits as the foundation of rights, a system of "negative liberties" and ordered constraints as the basis of freedom. In the constitutional philosophy, the possibilities of life, liberty and the pursuit of happiness are attainable only through a framework of neutral restraints—in economics, the discipline of the market; in politics, popular consent and the rule of law. This is the formula of liberal conservatism: the individual constrained by a government of laws; government limited by negative liberties. It is the formula of the constitutional founding. It is a wisdom reaffirmed by the catastrophes of the Left—of those who rejected this framework as a bourgeois concept and a mask for privilege— from the Jacobin Terror of the Eighteenth Century to the *gulags* built by Marxists two hundred years after.

The post-Communist Left also understands the significance of the Constitution as a bulwark of conservative principles and human freedoms. In his book, *Constitutional Faith,* radical law professor Sanford Levinson poses the question of whether progressives can even participate in America's social contract, whether they could "sign" the Constitution today in good faith. His answer is that they cannot. But radicals like Levinson are clever enough not to announce their subversive agendas so openly.[6] In order to justify a halfhearted "yes," and thus provide cover for his radical agendas, Levinson depreciates the Constitution as a document that crystallizes durable truths. Drawing on the "antifoundationalist" philosophy of Richard Rorty, he argues that the constitutional framework is merely a "discourse," a "linguistic system" in which virtually *any* social agenda can be expressed. According to Levinson, "[The Constitution] is less a series of propositional utterances than a commitment to taking political conversation seriously." It is a conversation, however, in which anything can be said.

Far from exhibiting an attitude that is eccentric or extreme, Levinson merely expresses the nihilistic temper of the contemporary Left. In *The Future of Liberal Revolution,* Yale law professor Bruce Ackerman even proposes a way of reading the Constitution so that a redistributionist agenda—one of the "wicked projects" that Madison's republic was designed to prevent—can be *incorporated* into its text. Extending this progressive argument, Mark Tushnet, of the Georgetown Law Center, suggests that one can employ what he calls "constitution-talk" to implement a program of affirmative rights and, indeed, the entire socialist agenda.[7]

Finding a radical flexibility in the constitutional text is necessary for radical law professors because the Constitution was clearly written to provide a conservative foundation for the American republic, establishing property as the basis of liberty and defending the autonomy of the individual against the claims of the state.

> Those who are well off [argues Levinson] might well be . . . appreciative of the Constitution's protection of so-called 'negative' liberties, that is rights against oppressive state interference in one's everyday life. . . . But what reason do persons mired in poverty have to be wildly appreciative of negative rights when what they seek are affirmative protections such as food, shelter, and clothing? . . . Might he or she . . . declare that a Constitution lacking a strongly affirmative Bill of Rights is not worth signing, whatever its other strengths might be?

Thus, the outlook of post-Communist progressives defines itself in denial of precisely the lesson that Twentieth-Century revolutions teach— that economic redistribution and affirmative rights, which form the basis of the socialist project, are inherently *anti*democratic and lead to the destruction of prosperity *and* justice *and* liberty—*for all.*

For the conservative, the Constitution is not a convenient discourse, but a repository of pragmatic and durable truths about liberty and prosperity in a social order. No one reading the argument of the Federalist Papers, which is an argument about the lessons of history, can fail to understand this. The truths embodied in the principles of the Constitution were validated for the founders by the experience of previously existing states. They have been confirmed in our lifetimes by the end results of the two-hundred-year war of the Left against the philosophical and political framework of "bourgeois" freedoms, against the idea of negative liberties and the practice of limited government, and by the Left's establishment of societies based on its own radical principles of positive freedoms—affirmative "rights" to food, shelter, employment and equality—and by the catastrophes they created.

In a famous afterword to *The Constitution of Liberty,* Hayek explained why he was not a conservative in the European sense. "Conservatism, proper," he wrote, "is a legitimate, probably necessary, and certainly widespread attitude of opposition to drastic change." It therefore cannot "offer an alternative to the direction in which we are moving." And that is a problem, given the dynamism of capitalist society, the openness of the American polity and the ascendance of radical ideology over the last half century.

While American radicals may have failed in their efforts to expropriate the means of material production, they have succeeded in appropriating enough of the means of cultural production to proclaim themselves "liberals" and to make the label stick. So ingrained have the premises of the Left become in the new liberal template, and so dominant is that template in the institutions of American culture, that conservatives now may be said to constitute a "counterculture." And that is another reason why conservatives must not think in strictly "conservative" terms when confronting the challenges before them. They must think of themselves as heirs to Locke and Burke and Madison, who faced a similar challenge from the Left of their time. Conservatives are, in fact, reformers demanding a universalist standard of one right, one law, one nation for all. They should be the champions of tolerance, and the opponents of group privilege and communal division. They must be the proponents of a common ground that is color-blind, gender-equitable and ethnically inclusive—of a government of laws that is neutral between its citizens, and limited in scope. For conservatives are the defenders of the free market against the destructive claims of the socialist agenda, and the conservers of the constitutional covenant against the forces of tyranny and the guardian state.

NOTES

INTRODUCTION: THE POLITICAL ARGUMENT REVIVED

1. Irving Kristol, *Neo-Conservatism* (New York, 1995), p. 486. For a survey of this ethos, cf. Robert H. Bork, *Slouching Towards Gomorrah: Modern Liberalism and American Decline* (New York, 1996).
2. Quoted in "Texas Observer No More" (a profile of Ronnie Dugger), *Los Angeles Times,* May 18, 1997.
3. Catharine MacKinnon, *Only Words* (Cambridge, Mass., 1993), p. 71.
4. For example, see Robin West, *Progressive Constitutionalism* (Durham, N.C., 1994); Gary Minda, *Post-Modern Legal Movements* (New York, 1995), pp. 169 ff; Kimberle Crenshaw et al., *Critical Race Theory* (New York, 1995); and Daniel A. Farber and Suzanna Sherry, *Beyond All Reason: The Radical Assault on Truth and Law* (Oxford, 1997).
5. Owen Fiss, *The Irony of Free Speech* (Cambridge, Mass., 1996), pp. 9, 12. "I am troubled by the attempt by Professor MacKinnon and others to work their way out of this conflict in ultimate values by defining liberty (in the form of free speech) out of the equation."
6. See discussion below, pp. 147 ff.
7. *Los Angeles Times,* December 17, 1996.
8. Opinion, U.S. Court of Appeals for the Ninth Circuit, Nos. 97-1530, 9715031; DC No. CV-96-4024-TEH, filed April 8, 1997. At one point in the conflict, Judith Winston, the Education Department's general counsel, made the following Orwellian remark to the *Los Angeles Times:* "Particular race-neutral criteria [such as tests] can have a discriminatory effect." Accord-

ing to the *Times*'s reporter, she was referring to the fact that "minority students as a group tend to score lower on standardized exams." Even this was incorrect, unless the minority was meant to exclude Asians and other minorities (e.g., Jews) who scored very well. *Los Angeles Times,* July 26, 1997.

9. Subsequently, the Ninth Circuit refused to review the issue *en banc,* and it was taken to the U.S. Supreme Court, where the plaintiffs were joined by liberal Harvard law professors Laurence Tribe and Kathleen Sullivan. The Supreme Court subsequently refused to review the case.

10. Peter Collier and David Horowitz, *Destructive Generation,* 2nd ed. (New York: 1996), p. 362; cf. also the comment of veteran leftist Stanley Aronowitz: "As the old Jules Feiffer cartoon goes, since liberals borrow their ideas from the left, when the left has no ideas neither do the liberals." Stanley Aronowitz, "Are They the Only Ones with New Ideas?: Why We Need a New Progressive Politics," *Social Policy,* vol. 27, no. 1 (Fall 1996). Allowing for its arrogance, the statement can be said to reflect a consensus that extends across the political spectrum.

11. See Friedrich Hayek, *The Mirage of Social Justice,* and the discussion below, chap. 6.

12. "Unnecessary Losses" was originally titled "Letter to a Political Friend," and is a chapter in *Destructive Generation.* "The Road to Nowhere" was printed in a modified and shortened version in *Commentary,* December 1990, under the title "Socialism: Guilty as Charged." "The Religious Roots of Radicalism" was first delivered in 1990 as a talk to the Pacific Jewish Center in Santa Monica under the title "The Fate of the Jews and the Radical Left."

1. THE LEFT AFTER COMMUNISM

1. Eric Hobsbawm, *Age of Extremes* (New York, 1995).

2. Joseph F. Keppler, *Seattle Times,* April 16, 1995.

3. *New York Times,* February 19, 1995.

4. *Los Angeles Times,* February 26, 1995.

5. Eugene D. Genovese, "The Squandered Century," *New Republic,* April 17, 1995.

6. E.g., "The failure of Soviet socialism does not reflect on the possibility of other kinds of socialism." Hobsbawm, op. cit., p. 498.

7. Similarly, North Korea was the industrial base of Korea until the advent of its Marxist regime. Yet South Korea, starting from an economic base lower than presocialist Cuba's, but thriving under capitalist incentives, became in four decades a First World industrial power, surpassing the Soviet Union itself.

8. Hobsbawm, op. cit., p. 403.

9. Ibid., p. 249.

10. Ibid.

11. Ibid., p. 250.

12. Ibid., p. 413.

13. Ibid., p. 416.

14. See the review essay by Fareed Zakaria in the *New Republic,* January 22, 1996.

15. "We are still left with that (now) unforgivable fact that some of the most socially concerned, hopeful-for-the-future, dedicated souls connived at the crimes in the Communist world, by refusing to recognise them and, then, by refusing to acknowledge them openly. Not ten, or a hundred, or a thousand, but many thousands, millions, all over the world. And this attitude— reluctance to criticise the Soviet Union, the great alma mater—goes on now and is shown by the way Hitler is put in the position of chief criminal of our times, whereas Stalin, a thousand times worse—and Hitler admired Stalin, quite properly seeing himself as a mere infant in crime compared to his great exemplar—is still handled gently in the imaginations of people on the left." Doris Lessing, *Walking in the Shade* (New York, 1997), p. 262.

16. Hilton Kramer, "The Counter-Revolution Abroad, The Cultural Revolution at Home," *New Criterion,* September 1991.

17. University of Massachusetts Professor Samuel Bowles, quoted in the *Wall Street Journal,* November 25, 1991.

18. E. J. Dionne, "'Who Won the Cold War?' New Left Historians Debate the Cold War," *Washington Post,* June 12, 1990.

19. Allan Bloom, *The Closing of the American Mind* (New York, 1987).

20. Private communication from Robert Boyers, editor of *Salmagundi,* November 18, 1991. Boyers was explaining his reasons for rejecting "The Road to Nowhere" (included in this volume) for his publication.

21. Richard Rorty, cited in Gertrude Himmelfarb, "Tradition and Creativity in the Writing of History," *First Things,* November 1992.

22. Cited by Marx in *The Eighteenth Brummaire,* in Karl Marx and Friedrich Engels, *Selected Writings,* vol. 1 (Moscow, 1962), p. 252.

23. Stephen Holmes, "The Permanent Structure of Antiliberal Thought," in Nancy L. Rosenblum, ed., *Liberalism and the Moral Life* (Cambridge, Mass., 1989).

24. Gene Veith, *Modern Fascism* (St. Louis, 1993), p. 12.

25. Harold Bloom, "Authority and Originality," in Mark Edmundson, ed., *Wild Orchids and Trotsky* (New York, 1993), p. 213. Or cf. Catharine

MacKinnon's description of her own intellectual process as an exercise in applying Marxism to gender issues, in *Toward a Feminist Theory of the State.*

26. David Denby, *Great Books* (New York, 1996), p. 24.

27. This is not to deny that the intellectual tradition of the Left has generated many critics of totalitarianism, like Arendt and Habermas on the above list. But they are not critics of the intellectual tradition whose paradigms produced these totalitarian results. One has only to compare *On the Origins of Totalitarianism* with Hayek's *Road to Serfdom* to appreciate the difference.

28. For examples of such claims, see Gerald Graff, *Beyond the Culture Wars,* and Lawrence Levine, *The Opening of the American Mind.*

29. Stanford University catalogue, 1997. The catalogue includes two other themes: "cross-cultural encounters" and "the impact of technology."

30. Cf. David Sacks and Peter Thiel, *The Diversity Myth: Multiculturalism and the Politics of Intolerance at Stanford* (Oakland, 1995). Sacks and Thiel were Stanford students who took this required course.

31. Ibid., p. 20, n. 20

32. Victor Farias, *Heidegger and Nazism* (Philadelphia, 1989), p. 191. Cf. also pp. 4–5, 220, 227, 253, 298.

33. Cited in Roger Kimball, "The Perversions of Michel Foucault," *The New Criterion,* vol. 11 (March 1993), p. 10.

34. Samuel Bowles, *Wall Street Journal,* November 25, 1991.

35. Cf. Leszek Kolakowski, *Main Currents of Marxism,* vol. 1 (Oxford, 1981), p. 130.

36. "The character of having value, when once impressed upon products, obtains fixity only by reason of their acting and re-acting upon each other as quantities of value. These quantities vary continually, independently of the will, foresight and action of the producers." Karl Marx, *Capital,* vol. 1 (Moscow, 1961), p. 75.

37. Ibid., p. 80

38. *The Nation,* December 11, 1989.

39. Robin West, *Progressive Constitutionalism: Reconstructing the Fourteenth Amendment* (Durham, N.C., 1994), pp. 17–18. West is a professor at the University of Georgetown Law Center. Cf. Farber and Sherry, op. cit.

40. By her own account, this would include critical legal studies, feminist legal studies, critical race studies and Marxist legal studies.

41. Quoted in Richard Rorty, "The Professor and the Prophet," *Transition,* no. 52, 1991.

42. Ibid.

43. Ibid.

44. Richard Rorty, "Unger, Castoriadis, and the Romance of a National Future" (1988), cited in Richard Posner, *Problems of Jurisprudence* (Cambridge, Mass., 1990), pp. 384–85.

45. Jeffrey C. Alexander and Stephen Jay Sherwood, "American Dream at a Turning Point," *Los Angeles Times*, September 15, 1991. Alexander is chairman of the sociology department at UCLA.

2. THE FATE OF THE MARXIST IDEA

1. Thomas Nagel, *The Last Word* (New York, 1996), p. 6.

2. Ludwig von Mises, *Socialism* (Indianapolis, 1981), p. 159.

3. Aileen Kraditor, *"Jimmy Higgins": The Mental World of the American Rank-and-File Communist, 1930–1958* (New York, 1988). "Jimmy Higgins" was a code for members of the Party's rank and file.

4. For testimonies of ex-radicals, see John H. Bunzel, ed., *Political Passages* (New York, 1988); Peter Collier and David Horowitz, eds., *Second Thoughts: Former Radicals Look Back at the Sixties* (Lanham, Md., 1989); and Peter Collier and David Horowitz, *Second Thoughts About Race* (Lanham, Md., 1990).

5. David Horowitz, *Radical Son* (New York, 1997), pp. 380–81, 398–401.

6. Carol Pasternak, a childhood friend. This letter originally appeared as a chapter of Peter Collier and David Horowitz, *Destructive Generation* 2nd ed., 1996 (New York, 1989).

7. "The Myth of Human Self-Identity" in Leszek Kolakowski and Stuart Hampshire, eds., *The Socialist Idea* (New York, 1974).

8. This was originally written as a letter to Ralph Miliband, an English Marxist, author of *Parliamentary Socialism* and other works, who was my mentor during the years I was in England, 1963–67. A revised and truncated version was published in *Commentary* magazine under the title "Socialism: Guilty as Charged." It has been restored to its original form and slightly altered for publication in this volume.

9. Marx, *Economic and Philosophical Manuscripts* (Moscow, 1961).

10. "The Crisis of Communist Regimes," *New Left Review*, September–October 1989. As New Left professor Michael Burawoy actually wrote in a special issue of *Socialist Review:* "Marxism is dead, long live Marxism!" "Now What? Responses to Socialism's Crisis of Meaning," *Socialist Review*, vol. 20, no. 2 (April–June 1990).

11. In commenting on the "sharpness of tone" in your review of Kolakowski's trilogy on Marxism, you explained: "I think this is in part attributable to a strong personal sense of disappointment at Kolakowski's political evolution. I have known Kolakowski since the fraught days of 1956 and have always thought him to be a man of outstanding integrity and courage, with a brilliant and original mind. His turning away from Marxism and, as I see it, from socialism has been a great boon to the reactionary forces of which he was once the dedicated enemy, and a great loss to the socialist cause, of which he was once the intrepid champion. I felt that loss very keenly. . . ." Ralph Miliband, *Class Power and State Power: Political Essays* (London, 1983), pp. 226–27.

12. Kolakowski, "The Priest and the Jester" (1959) in *Towards a Marxist Humanism* (New York, 1968).

13. Pinochet, it should be noted, received more votes from Chileans after fifteen years of dictatorial rule, than Salvador Allende—the Marxist he overthrew—had received in his own election.

14. Leszek Kolakowski, *Main Currents of Marxism,* 3 vols. (Oxford, 1978).

15. Ralph Miliband, "Kolakowski's Anti-Marx," *Political Studies,* vol. 29, no. 1 (1981). Kolakowski's reply, "Miliband's Anti-Kolakowski," is printed in the same issue. A revised version of Miliband's review is printed in Ralph Miliband, *Class Power and State Power.*

16. "At the core of Marxist politics, there is the notion of conflict [as] . . . civil war conducted by other means. [Social conflict] is not a matter of 'problems' to be 'solved' but of a state of domination and subjection to be ended by a total transformation of the conditions which give rise to it." Ralph Miliband, *Marxism and Politics* (Oxford, 1977), p. 17.

17. Cited in E. P. Thompson, *The Poverty of Theory* (New York, 1978), p. 345. For Kolakowski's analysis of the impossibility of nontotalitarian Marxist socialism, see "The Myth of Human Self-Identity" in Stuart Hampshire, ed. *The Socialist Idea* (New York, 1973). For Thompson's scholastic response to this argument, see Thompson, op. cit.

18. L. Trotsky, *In Defence of Marxism.* Cited in Isaac Deutscher, *The Prophet Outcast,* (Oxford, 1963), p. 468.

19. Isaac Deutscher, "The Meaning of De-Stalinization," in *Ironies of History* (Oxford, 1966), p. 21. Cf. Deutscher, *The Prophet Outcast,* p. 521: "Through the forcible modernization of the structure of society Stalinism had worked towards its own undoing and had prepared the ground for the return of classical Marxism."

20. Deutscher, "The Meaning of De-Stalinization," p. 58.

21. Deutscher, "Four Decades of the Revolution," in *Ironies of History,* p. 58.

22. Ibid.

23. Deutscher, "The Irony of History in Stalinism," (1958), in *Ironies of History.*

24. Isaac Deutscher, "Problems of Socialist Renewal: East and West," in *Socialist Register, 1988.*

25. Kolakowski, *Main Currents of Marxism,* vol. 1, *The Founders,* esp. chap. 1, "Origins of the Dialectic."

26. Miliband, "Kolakowski's Anti-Marx."

27. Zbigniew Brzezinski, *The Grand Failure* (New York, 1989), p. 237. For facts about Soviet society cited below, see also "Social and Economic Rights in the Soviet Bloc," special issue of *Survey,* August 1987; Richard Pipes, "Gorbachev's Russia: Breakdown or Crackdown?" *Commentary,* March 1990; Walter Laqueur, *The Long Road to Freedom: Russia and Glasnost* (New York, 1989); and *Wall Street Journal,* June 28, 1989.

28. Robert Heilbroner, "After Communism," *New Yorker,* September 10, 1990.

29. Murray Feshbach and Alfred Friendly, Jr., *Ecocide in the USSR* (New York, 1993). "No other great industrial civilization so systematically and so long poisoned its air, land, water and people. None so loudly proclaiming its efforts to improve public health and protect nature so degraded both. And no advanced society faced such a bleak political and economic reckoning with so few resources to invest toward recovery."

30. *The USSR in Figures for 1987* (Washington, D.C., 1988), p. 254.

31. Figures from Brzezinski, op. cit., p. 36, and George Gilder, "The American 80's," *Commentary,* September 1990. Gorbachev cited by Gilder.

32. Z (Martin Malia), "To the Stalin Mausoleum," *Daedalus,* Winter 1990.

33. A good post-Communist example of this mentality is on display in Benjamin Barber's jeremiad *Jihad vs. McWorld* (New York, 1966).

34. Robert Conquest, *The Harvest of Sorrow* (New York, 1986); Mikhail Heller and Aleksandr Nekrich, *Utopia in Power* (New York, 1986).

35. John Gray, "Totalitarianism, Reform and Civil Society," in *Totalitarianism at the Crossroads,* (Bowling Green, Ky., 1990).

36. Heller and Nekrich, op. cit., pp. 15–17

37. Isaac Deutscher, *The Prophet Unarmed: Trotsky 1921–1929* (New York, 1965), pp. 1–2. The internal quote refers to a passage from Machiavelli that Deutscher had used as an epigraph to *The Prophet Armed:* ". . . the nature of the people is variable, and whilst it is easy to persuade them, it is difficult to fix them in that persuasion. And thus it is necessary to take such measures that, when they believe no longer, it may be possible to make them believe by force."

38. Aleksandr Solzhenitsyn, *The Gulag Archipelago,* vol. 1, pp. 433 ff.

39. Ibid., p. 435n.

40. Sam Dolgoff, ed., *Bakunin on Anarchy* (New York, 1971), p. 319; emphasis in original.

41. Ludwig von Mises, op. cit.

42. John Gray, op. cit.; Friedrich Hayek, *The Constitution of Liberty; Law, Legislation and Liberty;* etc. Hayek's discussion of the calculation problem is included in vol. 10 of his collected works: *Socialism and War* (Chicago, 1997).

43. E. P. Thompson, op. cit.

44. Karl Marx, *Capital* (Moscow, 1961), p. 80.

45. Ibid., p. 72.

46. Isaac Deutscher, *The Prophet Outcast,* pp. 510–511.

3. THE RELIGIOUS ROOTS OF RADICALISM

1. First given as a lecture, "The Fate of the Jews and the Radical Left," at the Pacific Jewish Center, Santa Monica, 1991.

2. Isaac Deutscher, *The Non-Jewish Jew* (Oxford, 1968), p. 25.

3. Karl Marx in "On the Jewish Question." On the relation between Marx's Jewishness and his Marxism, see John Murray Cuddihy, *The Ordeal of Civility: Freud, Marx, Levi-Strauss, and the Jewish Struggle with Modernity* (New York, 1974); Julius Carlebach, *Karl Marx and the Radical Critique of Judaism* (Boston, 1978); and Paul Johnson, *A History of the Jews* (New York, 1987).

4. On the revolutionary roots of modern German anti-Semitism and Nazism, cf. Paul Lawrence Rose, *Revolutionary Antisemitism in Germany: From Kant to Wagner* (Princeton, N.J., 1990). On the socialist roots of fascism, see Ze'ev Sternhell, *The Birth of Fascist Ideology* (Princeton, N.J., 1994).

5. Cited in Mikhail Heller, *Cogs in the Wheel: The Formation of Soviet Man* (New York, 1988), p. 3.

6. Cf. Jan Valtin (pen name of Richard Herman Krebs), *Out of the Night* (New York, 1941). Krebs was a Comintern official: "Those who objected were threatened with expulsion from the Party. Discipline forbade the rank and file to discuss the issue. From then on, in spite of the steadily increasing fierceness of their guerrilla warfare, the Communist Party and the Hitler movement joined forces to slash the throat of an already tottering democracy."

7. Quoted in Robert S. Wistrich, *Revolutionary Jews from Marx to Trotsky* (New York, 1976), p. 207.

8. Louis Rappaport, *Stalin's War Against the Jews* (New York, 1990).

9. Wistrich, op. cit.

10. A radical magazine of the contemporary Left is even named *Tikkun*.

11. Eric Voegelin, *Science, Politics and Gnosticism* (Chicago, 1968); Irving Kristol, *Reflections of a Neo-Conservative*. On Marxism's roots in Christian mysticism, see Kolakowski, *Main Currents of Marxism*, vol. 1.

12. Cf. Cuddihy, op. cit.

13. Deuteronomy 30:15–18; 28:64; Leviticus 26:38.

14. H. H. Ben-Sasson, ed., *A History of the Jewish People*, (Cambridge, Mass., 1976), pp. 695ff.; Gershom Scholem, *Major Trends in Jewish Mysticism* (New York, 1961).

15. Gershom Scholem, *The Messianic Idea in Judaism* (New York, 1971), p. 87.

16. Scholem, *Major Trends in Jewish Mysticism*, p. 284.

17. Ibid., p. 297.

18. Marx, *Introduction to a Critique of Hegel's Philosophy of Right*. Cf. Kolakowski, *Main Currents of Marxism*, vol. 1: *The Founders*, pp. 127ff.

19. Cf. Paul Johnson, op. cit., pp. 352–53.

4. THE MEANING OF RIGHT AND LEFT

1. Cited in Isaiah Berlin, introduction to Joseph De Maistre, *Considerations on France* (Cambridge, England, 1994).

2. Of course, there was a tradition of democratic socialism before the Soviet fall. While the anti-Communist politics of these socialists were honorable enough, they nonetheless remained partisans of the Left, implacable critics of capitalist democracies and thus the most attractive promoters of a continuing socialist faith. By now, it should be evident even to them that a "democratic socialism" is a contradiction in terms.

3. Alec Nove, *The Economics of Feasible Socialism* (London, 1983). After the collapse of the Soviet Union, other texts appeared. For a summary and critique of market socialist theory, see David Ramsay Steele, "Immoral Capitalism vs. Unfeasible Socialism," *Critical Review* (Yale Station, Ct.), vol. 10, no. 3 (Summer 1996).

4. Cf. Friedrich Hayek, *The Mirage of Social Justice* (Chicago, 1976).

5. Of course, the socialist interpretation of the French Revolution, on which Harrington relied, has been thoroughly refuted on historical grounds in recent years in works by François Furet, Simon Schama and others.

6. Michael Harrington, *Socialism: Past and Future*, (New York, 1992), p. 5.

7. F. A. Hayek, *The Fatal Conceit: The Errors of Socialism* (Chicago, 1988), p. 6.

8. Hayek, *The Mirage of Social Justice*, pp. 133–34; cf. Hayek, *The Fatal Conceit*, chap. 1.

9. Lawrence Fuchs, cited in Arthur M. Schlesinger Jr., *The Disuniting of America* (Knoxville, Tenn., 1991), p. 79.

5. A RADICAL HOLOCAUST

1. Catharine MacKinnon, *Toward a Feminist Theory of the State* (Cambridge, Mass., 1991).
2. For examples, see Mary Lefkowitz, *Not Out of Africa* (New York, 1996).
3. Michael Warner, "Fear of a Queer Planet," *Social Text,* vol. 9, no. 4 (1991).
4. Kenneth Minogue, *Alien Powers: The Pure Theory of Ideology* (New York, 1985). This book is particularly rich in its analysis of feminism as a species of Marxism.
5. Catharine MacKinnon, op. cit. This is the "social constructivist" perspective that has become standard in academic women's studies and the feminist social sciences.
6. Randy Shilts, *And the Band Played On* (New York, 1995), p. 19.
7. Ibid., p. 20.
8. The most comprehensive survey of American sexuality reported that 67 percent of all men had only one lifetime partner, while only 9 percent of the entire sample of Americans said they had had more than twenty-one partners during their life. Robert T. Michael et al., *Sex in America: A Definitive Survey* (Boston, 1994). The statistics gathered for Kinsey's earlier survey are comparable. Rotello, *Sexual Ecology: AIDS and the Destiny of Gay Men* (New York, 1997).
9. Alan P. Bell and Martin S. Weinberg, *Homosexualities: A Study of Diversity Among Men and Women* (New York, 1978), cited in Rotello, op. cit., pp. 170–72.
10. Rotello, op. cit., p. 67
11. Shilts, op. cit., p. 39.
12. Michael Callen, *Surviving Aids* (New York, 1990), p. 4.
13. Ibid.
14. Ibid., pp. 5–6.
15. Shilts, op. cit., p. 39.
16. These and other disease statistics from Rotello, op. cit., p. 70.
17. Author's interview with Don Francis.
18. Quoted in Caleb Crain, "Pleasure Principles," *Lingua Franca,* October 1997.
19. Rotello, op. cit., pp. 72–73.
20. Ibid., p. 89.

21. "Sex and Sensibility," *The Advocate,* May 27, 1997.

22. Even nonmandatory testing efforts were thwarted at first. "HIV antibody testing became widely available in 1985, but initially most gay AIDS groups advised gay men to avoid the test." Rotello, op. cit., p. 107.

23. Ibid.

24. Ronald Bayer, *Private Acts, Social Consequences: AIDS and the Politics of Public Health* (New Brunswick, N.J., 1991).

25. Quoted in Shilts, op. cit., p. 220.

26. Rotello, op. cit. p. 86.

27. Author's interview with Don Francis.

28. The opposition to testing was based on the "civil rights" position that it would be an invasion of privacy and that the confidentiality of those tested would not be protected. This rested on false assumptions about government health practices in the past. When I interviewed Don Francis in the late Eighties, he told me, "We have been studying gay diseases since before Stonewall, and I don't know of a single case of breach of confidentiality." Yet mandatory confidential testing, which would allow public health officials to know where the infection was located and where it was spreading and to be able to warn those in its path, has been vigorously and successfully opposed by the gay community since the onset of the epidemic. I also asked Francis when he thought mandatory testing would finally be employed to fight the epidemic. He answered: "When enough people are dead." Cf. also Chandler Burr, "The AIDS Exception: Privacy vs. Public Health," *Atlantic Monthly,* June 1997.

29. Ibid.

30. Ibid.

31. Ralph Frerichs in Burr, op. cit.

32. Michael Fumento, *The Myth of Heterosexual AIDS* (New York, 1990), chap. 17.

33. Ibid., p. 243.

34. Ibid.

35. For this, and other examples, see Fumento, op. cit.

36. Rotello, op. cit. pp. 89–90.

37. Cf., for example, a report on the early handling of the epidemic by Peter Collier and myself, "AIDS: The Origins of a Political Epidemic," *California Magazine,* May 1983. Reprinted in Peter Collier and David Horowitz, *Deconstructing the Left* (Los Angeles, 1996).

38. Donald R. Hoover et al., "Estimating the 1978–1990 and Future Spread of Human Immunodeficiency Virus Type I in Subgroups of Homosexual

Men," *American Journal of Epidemiology,* vol. 134, no. 10 (1991), pp. 1190–1205.

39. Rotello, op. cit., p. 196.

40. Crain, op. cit.

41. Crain, op. cit., p. 202.

42. "In the Time of Love Controversy," *L.A. Weekly,* November 28, 1997.

43. Michael Bronski, "Sex in the '90s: The Problems of Pleasure," *Steam,* no. 2 (Summer 1994), pp. 132–34; Douglas Crimp, "How to Have Promiscuity in an Epidemic," in *October,* vol. 43 (Winter 1987), p. 253. Both citations in Rotello, op. cit., pp. 117, 203–4.

44. Rotello, op. cit., pp. 263–64.

6. A CONSERVATIVE HOPE

1. Cited in Albert O. Hirschmann, *The Rhetoric of Reaction* (Cambridge, Mass., 1991), pp. 1–3.

2. Hayek, *The Mirage of Social Justice* (Chicago, 1976), pp. 66–67.

3. Ibid., p. 69.

4. Garry Wills, "A Tale of Two Cities," *New York Review of Books,* October 3, 1996.

5. See above, p. 147.

6. Sanford Levinson, *Constitutional Faith* (Princeton, N.J., 1988), p. 190. And see Robin West, *Progressive Constitutionalism,* p. 168. Even though West believes that "the Constitution is methodologically and substantively hostile to progressive politics," she argues that it is a good idea to use the language of the text to frame progressive agendas as a way of making it more palatable to opponents. See chap. 7, "Constitutional Skepticism."

7. Levinson, op. cit., p. 192.

ACKNOWLEDGMENTS

MY THANKS TO Eve Burud for her meticulous and patient preparation of the manuscript; to Chad Conway of The Free Press for his solicitous attention to details and requests both necessary and unnecessary; to Adam Bellow; and to my agent Georges Borchardt.

INDEX

academy, the. *See* universities
Ackerman, Bruce, 186–87
activist judges, 11
Adam and Eve, 125–26
affirmative action, 8–12
Afro-centrism, 156
Age of Extremes (Hobsbawm), 18–26
AIDS: anal sex as primary path of
 transmission, 167, 173; blood
 donor screening for HIV, 169–70,
 199n.22; classification as sexually
 transmitted disease, 171; and core
 group sexual activity, 166, 167,
 170, 175; cure for, 175, 177; deaths
 in the U.S., 178; de-gaying of,
 173; education on controlled by
 gay leaders, 172–74; epidemic in
 homosexual community, 172–73;
 and gay liberation, 164–78; heterosexual epidemic myth, 173–74;
 HIV testing, 171, 199n.28; HIV
 virus transmission, 166–67; the
 Left as dominating handling of, 2;
 "magic bullets" for, 175, 177; national policy on as progressive,
 174–75; number of Americans infected with HIV, 172; Paglia on re-

sponsibility for, 155; research on,
 175; safe sex for preventing,
 175–76; second wave of, 176
"AIDS: The Origins of a Political
 Epidemic" (Collier and
 Horowitz), 199n.37
alienation, 124–25
Allende, Salvador, 194n.13
Althusser, Louis, 33, 91
American Civil Liberties Union
 (ACLU): in California Civil
 Rights Initiative suit, 9; HIV test-
 ing opposed by, 171
American Revolution, 142
Americans for Democratic Action,
 4–5
Amidah, 128
amoebiasis, 162
antifoundationalism, 31, 186
anti-Semitism: on the Left, 123; in
 Marx, 120; on the Right, 120,
 123; socialism elevating to global
 principle, 136; in socialism's
 founders, 120
Arendt, Hannah, 34, 192n.27
Aron, Raymond, 34, 46
Aronowitz, Stanley, 190n.10

203